Encountering Ecclesiastes

Encountering Ecclesiastes

A Book for Our Time

James Limburg

William B. Eerdmans Publishing Company

Grand Rapids, Michigan / Cambridge, U.K.

© 2006 James Limburg
All rights reserved

Published 2006 by
Wm. B. Eerdmans Publishing Co.
255 Jefferson Ave. S.E., Grand Rapids, Michigan 49503 /
P.O. Box 163, Cambridge CB3 9PU U.K.
www.eerdmans.com

Printed in the United States of America

11 10 09 08 07 06   7 6 5 4 3 2 1

Library of Congress Cataloging-in-Publication Data

Limburg, James, 1935-
    Encountering Ecclesiastes : a book for our time / James Limburg.
       p.   cm.
    Includes bibliographical references and index.
    ISBN-10: 0-8028-3047-1 / ISBN-13: 978-0-8028-3047-0 (pbk.: alk. paper)
    1. Bible. O.T. Ecclesiastes — Commentaries. I. Title.

BS1475.53.L56 2006
223′.807 — dc22

                                        2006010895

Unless otherwise noted, the Scripture quotations in this publication are from the New
Revised Standard Version of the Bible, copyright © 1989 by the Division of Christian Education of the National Council of Churches of Christ in the U.S.A., and used by permission, or from the Good News Translation — Second Edition © 1992, American Bible Society, and used by permission.

In memory of my grandparents, whom I never knew

Miko Groote (1876-1916)

Elsena Ahrenholz Groote (1875-1920)

They kept the farm, and kept the faith.

For our grandchildren

Kai, Mara, Elin, Benjamin and Eleyna

"The world endures only because of the breath (Hebrew *hevel*) of school children."

The Talmud, *Shabbat* 119b

Contents

PREFACE   ix

ABBREVIATIONS   xiv

1. What's It All About?   1
   Getting Into Ecclesiastes

2. Is That All There Is?   21
   Ecclesiastes 1–2

3. Who Knows?   36
   Ecclesiastes 3

4. "Who's Been Working the Hardest?"   53
   Ecclesiastes 4

5. What About God?   66
   Ecclesiastes 5

6. What About Death?   84
   Ecclesiastes 6 and 7

Contents

7. So How Should I Live My Life?   103
   Ecclesiastes 9, 11, 12:1-8

8. What It's All About   124
   Ecclesiastes for Our Time

BIBLIOGRAPHY OF WORKS CITED   139

Preface

Vielleicht ist es doch ein Schlag ins Wasser!
(Maybe it'll be a flop!)

> Gerhard von Rad on his book
> *Weisheit in Israel (Wisdom in Israel),* 1970

Leichen Text: Pred. 7,2 (Funeral text: Ecclesiastes 7:2)
"It is better to go to the house of mourning than to go to the house of feasting;
for this is the end of everyone, and the living will lay it to heart."

> Inscription on the tombstone of my maternal grandfather

"Of making many books there is no end," the writer of Ecclesiastes once observed. Certainly this is true. Therefore, if someone is writing a book, especially a book dealing with Ecclesiastes, the reader has a right to know what the author is up to, and why.

This book is the result of a pair of experiences in my own life. First, there was a conversation with Gerhard von Rad, professor of Old Testament in Heidelberg, Germany. I had been taking classes in Old Testament in Heidelberg during the summer semester of 1970.

Gerhard von Rad had retired, but was still living in the area. I wrote to him, asking if I could visit him at his home when the semester was over in July, when I knew my German would be as good as it was going to get. I also asked if I could tape record our conversation, as a greeting for my students at Augustana College in South Dakota.

Von Rad sent a postcard in immediate response, inviting me for coffee on a weekday morning and adding, "Bitte, Verzichten Sie die Sache mit dem Tape Recorder!" ("Please forget the business with the tape recorder!").

I arrived at the von Rad home in Handschuhsheim on a July morning and was warmly welcomed by the professor and his wife. We drank coffee and talked about Old Testament subjects for a memorable couple of hours. I recall being struck by the fact that he was much interested in how we went about teaching the Old Testament to college students in America. Then I asked what he was currently working on, and he told me of his book on wisdom literature in the Bible, which was to appear later that year. Then he added, "Vielleicht ist es doch ein Schlag ins Wasser!" which may be freely translated, "Maybe it'll be a flop!" Those who know anything about von Rad, and about that book, know that what the professor said that day was wrong. The book went on to become a great success and was quickly translated into a variety of modern languages.

I ordered the book and received it a few weeks after we arrived home in America. I went through it immediately and was especially intrigued by the section dealing with Ecclesiastes. In the fall of 1971, I began teaching a unit on Ecclesiastes in my Freshman Bible course. That same fall, when we faculty members were invited to offer three-session study seminars in our homes for colleagues, the group that gathered at our home read Ecclesiastes together. Taking part were professors from the faculties of nursing, physics, biology, chemistry, history, English, and religion, making for a lively discussion experience. What I essentially did in these classes and in this faculty seminar was to offer an Americanized and expanded version of von Rad's approach to Ecclesiastes.

The second memorable experience with Ecclesiastes took place

Tombstone of Miko Groote, 1876-1916
Emden, Minnesota, Cemetery

the following spring. In April 1972, my mother's sister died, and our
family converged at a small country cemetery near Renville, Minnesota, for the burial. It was cold and rainy. My mother told us that it
had been the same kind of weather when her father had died at 39
and was buried in this cemetery; she was just eight years old.

After the graveside ceremony, I walked away, alone in the drizzle,
looking at the tombstones in that cemetery. The earliest were from

the 1860s, with some inscriptions in Dutch and some in German, reflecting the congregation's history. "They preached in German in the morning and Dutch in the afternoon," my mother had explained to me. But after 1920 or so, all the inscriptions were in English.

Then I saw it: my grandfather's tombstone. I had seen it during earlier visits to the grave as a child, but had not remembered much about it. I subtracted the dates and confirmed that he had died at age 39. There was his name and then the inscription: "Leichen Text: Pred. 7,2." I knew that Pred. was the abbreviation for *Prediger,* meaning "Preacher," which was the name for the book of Ecclesiastes in the German Bible. But I didn't know just what that biblical text said.

When we got back to an uncle's house, I looked up the text in a King James Version of the Bible: "It is better to go to the house of mourning, than to go to the house of feasting: for that is the end of all men; and the living will lay it to his heart." I wondered: What would that preacher have said, based on that text, to comfort a young widow and two little girls on that rainy day so long ago?

The next week, I was responsible for preaching in chapel at the college. I pulled out the Bible and von Rad's new book and prepared a chapel talk on Eccl 7:2. During the next few years, whenever I was asked to teach in a congregation, or lead a discussion for pastors, or speak at a church convention, I tried to deal with a text from Ecclesiastes. And each year in my introductory Freshman Bible class, we spent four or five sessions on Ecclesiastes, which captured the interest, I discovered, of these 18-year-old college students.

Soon after accepting a call to teach at Luther Seminary in St. Paul, I began offering a seminar on Ecclesiastes, working through the Hebrew and Greek texts. That seminar continued during my teaching at Pacific Lutheran Seminary in Berkeley. We listened to music based on Ecclesiastes ("Turn, Turn, Turn") or dealing with themes introduced there ("Is that all there is?"). We studied what Luther, Bonhoeffer, and others have said about Ecclesiastes, and noted the role the book plays in the Jewish festival of Sukkot. Thus the materials gathered here have grown directly out of a variety of teaching and preaching situations: at a college, two seminaries, at lay schools of theology, as a six-part series of Lenten sermons in a congregation, at synod assemblies, and faculty discussion groups.

As I write these words, I am looking out at one of Minnesota's most beautiful lakes. I remain grateful to parents and grandparents who kept the family farm as an inheritance for our generation, and who have kept the faith and passed it on to the rest of us, even through an inscription on a tombstone. Finally, I wish to thank many who helped and encouraged me along the way. First, there are students from Augustana College, Luther Seminary, Pacific Lutheran Seminary, and schools of the Graduate Theological Union in Berkeley, who raised questions, brought recordings and videos to the classes, and discussed every aspect of the book. Editor Reinder van Til has tirelessly offered encouragement and criticism and has been a faithful conversation partner. Thanks are due especially to Martha, who has enabled me to "enjoy life with the wife whom you love" (Eccl 9:9) for a half century now.

Summer, 2005
Woman Lake, Minnesota

Abbreviations

CEV   Contemporary English Version

JPS   Jewish Publication Society Version

KJV   King James Version

NIV   New International Version

NRSV   New Revised Standard Version

RSV   Revised Standard Version

TEV   Today's English Version

1 What's It All About?
Getting Into Ecclesiastes

The book thus shows the low-water mark of God-fearing Jews in pre-Christian times.

Assessment of Ecclesiastes in J. R. Dummelow, ed.,
A Commentary on the Holy Bible (1952), p. 391

For many modern agnostics this book is the last bridge to the Bible. Some Christians today find in Qoheleth a kind of back door — at once sinister and highly esteemed — through which their minds can admit those skeptical and melancholy sentiments that would be refused entry at portals where cultivation of virtue and belief in the afterlife are inscribed on the lintel.

Norbert Lohfink, *Qoheleth* (2003), p. 1

This book, which on many counts deserves to be in everyone's hands and to be familiar to everyone . . . has until now been deprived of its reputation and dignity and has lain in miserable neglect, so that today we have neither the use nor the benefit from it that we should.

Martin Luther, *Notes on Ecclesiastes* (1526), p. 7

E cclesiastes is not for everyone.

Should a new convert to Christianity come to me, wanting to take instruction in preparation for joining a Christian community, I think we would begin by reading the Gospel of John (to get the Good News or Gospel straight), then move to a study of some Psalms (to learn how to pray and praise), and then to the Letter to the Ephesians (to consider some biblical pictures of the church). Or if members of the social action committee in a congregation asked about biblical resources to inform their social concern, I would suggest reading Amos or the first part of Isaiah. For those wanting to stoke the fires for mission in the congregation, I would propose that we start with the book of Jonah and then move to a study of the book of Acts in the New Testament.

But I think of others, especially students at all levels, from high school to retirement age, who have had more than enough of sermons, Sunday School, church services, and religious instruction. Or there may be some honest doubters, questers, those looking for answers to the mysteries about God, the world, and human suffering. There may be a college student who senses that the foundations of a childhood faith are shaking, and who is haunted by doubts. Or another student who shows up at a professor's or pastor's office and says, "I just can't pray any more." To such persons I have said, and will continue to say, "Have you ever read Ecclesiastes? Let's take a look at it together."

Ecclesiastes is not helpful for everyone. But it does have an honest, invigorating, often surprising word for many persons. Imagine that you live in a beautiful city and are entertaining guests from another country. You want to introduce them to some of your favorite places in your city. You visit an art center and a museum. You show them the concert hall where the symphony performs and the sports dome where the football and baseball teams play. You walk with them around one of the lakes and stroll down the streets of a shopping mall.

But certain guests — only certain special guests whom you know well — you take to another place. Near the University, on a back street, is a favorite bookstore. This is not a megastore with thousands of books and a coffee house attached. This is a small shop run by a book lover who is a somewhat eccentric, shadowy figure, who moves in and out of piles of books that are stacked in no apparent order. Your guest discovers a particularly fine volume to add to his collection of sea stories. You continue your search for a novel to complete your collection of books by Peter DeVries. And so on.

Now, let us say that you are a teacher, and your assignment is to introduce students to "the strange new world of the Bible," to use Karl Barth's phrase. It will be important that they hear the accounts of Creation in Genesis, the call for justice in the prophets, the prayers and praise in the Psalms, the Good News in the New Testament. And so, year by year, you faithfully teach those great biblical texts. But every once in a while you meet a student who has "been there and done that." Perhaps she has been turned off by too many tiresome sermons, too many slides of the Holy Land, too much of what seems to be dishonest religion. For her, the Bible is not a "strange new world," but a somewhat familiar, even somewhat boring one. Or there may be a reluctant student who would rather be enrolled in Philosophy 101 but who is taking your course only because it is a graduation requirement and fits his schedule. Or perhaps there's an honest quester, seeking answers to questions about God and life and death.

Over decades of teaching, I've encountered such students. They've been among my favorites. If you should find yourself among those described above, I say to you, "Come along with me to a favorite place of mine. It's a bit offbeat. It's that little bookshop, just around the corner. The sign above the door? It says 'Ecclesiastes.' It's not everyone's cup of tea. But who knows? You might find it interesting!"

Mixed Reviews

The biblical book of Ecclesiastes has always received mixed reviews by biblical scholars. Consider the following:

3

Other scholars too are forced to admit how lukewarm his faith really is, and how far he falls below the higher peaks of Old Testament piety.

> Walter Baumgartner on Ecclesiastes, in H. H. Rowley, ed.,
> *The Old Testament and Modern Study,* p. 225

The book has indeed the smell of the tomb about it.

> H. Wheeler Robinson, *Inspiration and Revelation*
> *in the Old Testament,* p. 258

Taken together with the words from J. R. Dummelow above, these citations give a sampling of the attitude of biblical scholarship toward Ecclesiastes at the middle of the 20th century.

But now, at the beginning of the 21st century, there is a new interest and appreciation for Ecclesiastes. In addition to the quotation from Lohfink cited above, consider the following:

> The book of Qoheleth or Ecclesiastes has become timely again today, when horizons are closing in and the present becomes a hard master, demanding sacrifices and suppressing dreams. . . . We see Qoheleth's wise sayings as rays of light, shining through the cracks in a dark, depressing room.
>
> Elsa Tamez (Costa Rica), *When the Horizons Close,* p. v

> In focusing our attention on this life rather than the next, indeed, this book contributes to the correction of an all-too-frequent imbalance throughout the ages in Christian thinking, which has sometimes presented Christianity as if it were more a matter of waiting for something than a matter of living.
>
> Iain Provan (British Columbia),
> *Ecclesiastes/Song of Songs,* p. 42

No adolescent could be more scathing of the delusions under which her successful and success-driven parents labor. For this rea-

4

son, the book has a special appeal for youth of high school and college age, as well as for young adults struggling with the disappointment of "the real world."

Ellen F. Davis (Durham, North Carolina),
Proverbs, Ecclesiastes, and the Song of Songs, p. 161

In the Bibliography I have listed more than a dozen recent commentaries on Ecclesiastes. Each is worth studying, and each has a positive evaluation of that biblical book. For a complete listing of recent commentaries and studies on Ecclesiastes (Eccl 12:12b!), see the commentaries of Fox, Horne, and Krüger listed there; search also "Ecclesiastes" on the Internet, which lists more than 200,000 entries.

Church and Synagogue

While there is a great deal of interest concerning Ecclesiastes in recent scholarship, the book receives scant attention in lectionary-directed preaching and in the liturgy of the churches. The *Revised Common Lectionary* is used to guide preaching in Roman Catholic, Episcopalian, Lutheran, and other denominational bodies, assigning preaching texts for each Sunday of the year. This lectionary assigns texts from Ecclesiastes only for the Sunday closest to August 3, Year C (Eccl 1:12-14 and 2:[1-7, 11] 18-23), and for New Year's Eve, Years ABC (Eccl 3:1-13). A churchgoer could attend worship services for years and hardly hear a word out of the book of Ecclesiastes from the lectern or the pulpit. The daily lectionary readings, however, designed to guide private reading of Scripture, schedule readings through the entire book during the weeks of 3 and 4 Pentecost (*Lutheran Book of Worship,* p. 189).

Of course there have been and continue to be exceptions, where individuals choose to preach on this book independent of any lectionary directives. A striking example: in January 2001, I had occasion to visit the amazing Herzog August Library in Wolfenbüttel, Germany, under the guidance of a faculty colleague doing research there and the library's research librarian. While paging through a number of ancient tomes on Ecclesiastes, we discovered a two-volume collection of sermons on that book, published in 1642. These volumes, totaling 1,930 pages, contain some 120 sermons, preached over a period of more than two years in the cathedral in Ulm, Germany, by one Cunrad Dietrich. The sermons were delivered weekly. Sometimes, because of their length, sermons continued over two Sundays. Many times there were two sermons on one verse of Ecclesiastes, but most often the sermons dealt with several verses. One marvels at the skill of any preacher, ancient or modern, who could sustain the interest of a congregation for such a series! When one considers this and other ancient commentaries on Ecclesiastes, as well as the fact that today one can instantly locate hundreds of thousands of books and studies of Ecclesiastes with the help of an internet search engine, one has a new appreciation for the biblical comment about there being no end to the making of many books (Eccl 12:12)![1]

If Ecclesiastes is largely neglected in formal worship settings in the churches, the situation is quite different in Judaism. The book of Ecclesiastes, or Qoheleth as it is called in Hebrew, is read aloud each year as the biblical text for the Jewish festival of Sukkoth, celebrated in the fall (see Chapter 7 below). This practice, structured into the normal cycle of the worship year, has kept the book alive and well-read, or at least well-heard, in the Jewish tradition. Three important recent works by Jewish scholars should be mentioned: the commentaries by Robert Gordis and by Michael V. Fox and the popular book by Rabbi Harold Kushner, *When All You've Ever Wanted Isn't Enough*.

---

1. For an enlightening survey of both Jewish and Christian scholarship on Ecclesiastes from the pre-Christian era through 1860, see C. D. Ginsburg, *The Song of Songs and Coheleth* (1861; repr. New York: Ktav, 1970). Ginsburg reports on an exposition of Ecclesiastes by a Jesuit commentator, Pineda, in 1620 which ran 1,079 pages. This "gigantic commentary" (130) is of value in supplying "a thorough digest . . . of all the Fathers and others have said upon each verse" (124).

Popular Culture and Piety

Certain portions of the book of Ecclesiastes continue to appear in popular culture and popular piety. The most well-known part of the book is the poem about the "times" in Ecclesiastes 3. In its musical setting by Pete Seeger (1954) and performed by The Byrds (and others), it became a part of the cultural protest against the war in Viet Nam in the 1960s. The song continues to be recorded, sung, played, quoted, and illustrated in contexts where people express longing for a "time of peace" (see Chapter 3 below).

Quotations from the book also appear in everyday life. A few personal examples: I recall visiting with an older Christian in her 80s who told me that she had had words from Eccl 12:12 posted above her desk in a dormitory room of an Iowa college: "Much study is a weariness of the flesh." Once I noted words from Eccl 9:7 printed at the top of the menu in a South Dakota restaurant : "Go, eat your bread with enjoyment, and drink your wine with a merry heart." I have already commented on the use of Eccl 7:2 for a grandfather's funeral text (see the Preface and Chapter 6 below). While rummaging through some old scrapbooks, I discovered the church bulletin for June 4, 1949, the day of my confirmation in the Lutheran Church in our town. On the cover of the bulletin is a well-known picture of the boy Jesus at age 12. Under the picture, printed in elegant Gothic type, is the text of Eccl 12:1-7, directed to us confirmands: "Remember your creator in the days of your youth . . ." (see Chapter 7 below). The reader can supply his or her own examples of further quotations from Ecclesiastes that appear in ordinary, everyday contexts.

Though Ecclesiastes has often been neglected in the preaching and teaching of the church, there have also been times when this small book, or portions of it, has spoken loudly and clearly to a particular situation. We have already mentioned the words about "a time for peace" in connection with the Viet Nam war. We shall comment on some other instances in the pages that follow. To cite two examples: Martin Luther's lectures on Ecclesiastes in the 16th century at the time of the Reformation had powerful effects, and continue to be useful in pointing the way for the interpretation and relevance of the book for our time (see below). In the 20th century, Dietrich Bonhoeffer referred to Ecclesiastes often, in sermons, books, and letters (see Chapter 3 below).

Elias Bickerman has named Ecclesiastes one of the "Four Strange Books of the Bible," in his book with that title. So what is this "strange book" really all about? Is it indeed a tedious and tepid recital of a faith that is "lukewarm" (Baumgartner)? Is it a musty tome reeking of the "stench of the tomb" (Robinson)? Or is it an invitation to earthly happiness and to radical involvement in the issues of this world (Bonhoeffer; see Chapter 3 below)? Is it a call to flee from the world and its distractions (Jerome; see below)? Or does it intend to encourage readers to "happily enjoy the things that are present . . . lest we permit the present moment, our moment, to slip away" (Luther)?

In Ecclesiastes 3, the writer speaks eloquently about doing things at the right time. And now, it would appear, is the right time to turn to the book itself.

The Pedal Point (Ecclesiastes 1:1-2)

> [1]The words of the Teacher, the son of David, king in Jerusalem.
> [2]Vanity of vanities, says the Teacher, vanity of vanities! All is vanity.

Authorship and Setting

Who wrote the book of Ecclesiastes? The reference to the "son of David" suggests Solomon, David's son (2 Sam 12:24-25) who was king in Jerusalem from about 961 to 922 B.C.E. A number of biblical and deuterocanonical books are associated with Solomon (see Prov 1:1; 10:1; 25:1; Song 1:1). But here, in Ecclesiastes, Solomon is not mentioned by name. The reference to "all who were before me in Jerusalem" in 2:9 would seem strange coming from Solomon, since there was only one king in Jerusalem before Solomon, namely David. Such observations, as well as the fact that the Hebrew language of the book is more characteristic of a period much later than King Solomon, all suggest that the reference to "the son of David" is a literary device linking the book of Ecclesiastes to Solomon, the great figure from Israel's past remembered for his wisdom (1 Kgs 3; 4:29-34), but not actually claiming him as author. Most scholars believe that the book was written around 250 B.C.E., in Jerusalem (note the reference to the temple there in 5:1).

If this mid-3rd century date is correct, what was the situation of those living in and around Jerusalem at this time? During the days of King David and King Solomon in the 10th century, Israel had been the ranking nation in the eastern Mediterranean world. But then came the split of the kingdom in 922 into Israel and Judah, the fall of Israel to the Assyrians in 722 and of Judah to the Babylonians in 587. A good many of the Jews were deported to Babylon, living there in exile from 587 until 539, when the Persians conquered that city and allowed them to return to Jerusalem and Judah. The Jews lived under Persia rule until 332, when the armies of Alexander the Great moved eastward and "the world became Greek overnight," as historians have put it. The consensus of contemporary scholars, then, is that the writer of Ecclesiastes was a Jew living in Jerusalem during the period of Greek rule, when the Jewish community was but a small island in the vast sea of the Greek empire.

What would have been the mood of the Jewish people living there? What were their thoughts about God? They had heard, of course, about the mighty acts of God in the past glory days of their nation, from the time of Abraham and Sarah through the Exodus from Egypt, the wanderings in the wilderness, the conquest of the land of Palestine, and the monarchy under David, Solomon, and all the rest. But judging from the hard realities of life in the 3rd century, God appeared not to be doing many "mighty acts" in their day! These citizens of Jerusalem had heard of the powerful words that God had spoken through prophets like Amos, Hosea, Isaiah, and Jeremiah in the past, but God seemed not to be saying much in their present time! We assume that it was in such a situation, where God

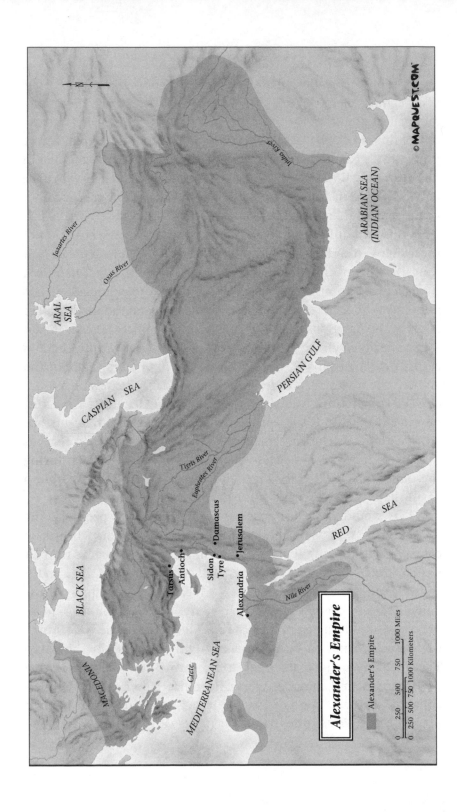

Alexander's Empire

Alexander's Empire

0   250   500   750   1000 Miles
0 250 500 750 1000 Kilometers

ARABIAN SEA
(INDIAN OCEAN)

Indus River

Iaxartes River

Oxus River

ARAL SEA

PERSIAN GULF

CASPIAN SEA

Tigris River

Euphrates River

RED SEA

Damascus
Jerusalem

Antioch
Tarsus
Sidon
Tyre
Alexandria

Nile River

BLACK SEA

MACEDONIA

Crete

MEDITERRANEAN SEA

N

© MAPQUEST.COM

seemed far removed and silent, that the author of Ecclesiastes lived and worked.

The author of the book is named "the Teacher" in the NRSV translation (1:1, 2, 12; 7:27; 12:8, 9, 10). In the original Hebrew the word is *Qoheleth* (NRSV footnote), which means a person who teaches in the *qahal* or "assembly" of the people (see Deut 31:30). While older Bibles translated the word as "Preacher" (KJV; German *Prediger*), it is best translated as "Teacher" or transliterated as "Qoheleth" (NRSV note to 1:1, etc.) or "Koheleth" (JPS translation). In any case, in the passages cited above, the author describes his work as that of a teacher, not of a king like Solomon. The apocryphal book of Sirach presents the words of a "wise person" in Jerusalem, who wrote sometime between about 200 and 180 B.C.E. Sirach's description of his own vocation also fits that of Qoheleth: "A wise person instructs his own people, and the fruits of his good sense will endure" (Sir 37:23).

Theme

"Vanity of vanities . . . all is vanity." This sentence strikes the theme for the book. The Hebrew word translated as "vanity" is *hevel* (rhymes with English "level"). The literal meaning of the word is "breath" (Isa 57:13 NRSV; JPS translates "breeze"). The word occurs with its literal meaning in the Talmud: "The world endures only because of the breath [*hevel*] of school children" (*b. Šabb.* 119b, Gordis, p. 205; see the dedication to this book). When I have taught the book of Ecclesiastes in a classroom, at this point I reach into a pocket and pull out a cigar. I carefully remove the cellophane wrapper, strike a match, light the cigar, take a deep draw, and blow out a puff of smoke. "That," I say, "is something like what the writer of Ecclesiastes means when he says *hevel*. It means a breath, a vapor, a cloud of steam, like a puff of smoke. Observe two things about that puff of smoke: (1) It is without substance. You can't grab onto it. (2) It is not lasting. Now we see the puff of smoke; in a few seconds we will no longer be able to detect it." (I notice that in *The Message*, Eugene Peterson translates *hevel* throughout Ecclesiastes as "smoke.")

Most often, *hevel,* which occurs 70 times in the Bible, is used in a figurative way, indicating the brevity and insignificance of human life: "my life is a breath" (Job 7:7, also 16; see also Ps 39:5 and context: "Surely everyone stands as a mere breath"; 62:9 twice; 78:33: "So he made their days vanish like a breath"; 144:4). In sum, when human life is called or compared to *hevel,* two things are being said: (1) life is empty, without substance or significance; (2) life is transitory, not lasting. Thus there are both a qualitative and quantitative dimension to the meaning of the word.

Finally, *hevel is* translated as "Abel," the son of Adam and Eve, in Genesis 4. Claus Westermann observes, "At the beginning of the Old Testament there is an allusion to the transitory character of man in this name Abel; at the end, in the leading theme of Ecclesiastes [Ecclesiastes is one of the last books in the ordering of the Hebrew Bible]" (*Handbook to the Old Testament,* p. 246).

In sum, *hevel* is the thematic word for the book of Ecclesiastes. It can be translated into English as "breath," "vanity," "nothing," "nothingness," "useless." Thirty-seven out of some 70 occurrences in the entire Bible occur in Ecclesiastes. The expression *"hevel* of *hevels"* ("vanity of vanities") frames the book (1:2 and 12:8). In the pages that follow, I will most often follow the NRSV translation (usually "vanity") unless there is reason to translate *hevel* differently for the sake of a more precise understanding of the Hebrew original.

Finally, Gerhard von Rad comments on *hevel:*

In contrast with the older wisdom teachers, Qoheleth has stepped over a boundary which they — for whatever reasons — did not cross. While they did not try to formulate any abstractions summarizing the meaning of life, Qoheleth immediately goes after the whole. He lumps all of life's experiences together and then labels the sum "nothingness" *(hevel).* Like a pedal-point [a sustained bass note running through an organ composition or portion of a composition] this word runs through the entire book.

Weisheit in Israel, p. 304, my translation

To illustrate the point that von Rad is making, take the plainsong hymn, "Of the Father's Love Begotten" (*Psalter Hymnal* 342; see p. 14). Have those who sing bass sing "loo" on an E flat and sustain that note. Let the other voices sing the melody line, with words or singing "loo." That sustained E flat is a pedal point which would, of course, be played on an organ.[2] Now, as you read through the book of Ecclesiastes, listen for that pedal point that labels so many things as *hevel*. Imagine the meaning of that word as a breath, a vapor, even a puff of smoke. And translate it as "nothing, nothingness, vanity" according to what the context requires.

The "Story" in Ecclesiastes

The book of Ecclesiastes is not a narrative, like the stories in the biblical books of Ruth or Esther or Jonah. There is, however, a progression of thought running through it, and we do well to begin by getting a sense of that progression which we shall call the "story" the book tells.

The theme is struck in 1:2, with the fivefold repetition of the word "vanity," translating Hebrew *hevel*. As we have seen, the literal meaning of the word is a breath of air. In Ecclesiastes the word is always used in a figurative sense, indicating something that is without substance and not lasting. For the sake of this story we shall leave it untranslated, as *hevel*. Wherever we are in the story, that word *hevel* is always sounding in the background, like a sustained bass note on an organ.

Ecclesiastes 1 and 2

The story begins with the author reporting on his quest to discover what life is all about. He has tried to find life's meaning in his work, or in learning, or in pleasure. But none of these efforts is ultimately

2. Thanks to church organist Carol Hokel for this illustration.

Of the Father's Love Begotten

Aurelius Clemens Prudentius

Of the Fa-ther's love be-got-ten Ere the worlds be-gan to be, He is Al-pha and O-me-ga,

Loo

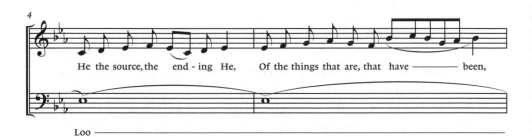

He the source, the end-ing He, Of the things that are, that have been,

Loo

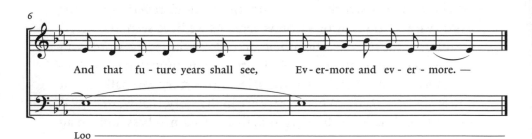

And that fu-ture years shall see, Ev-er-more and ev-er-more. —

Loo

"Of the Father's Love Begotten," Plainsong melody;
treble line from Koester, *Revelation and the End of All Things,* p. 33

satisfying. He decides that the best way to live in these circumstances is to find enjoyment in the company of friends, in the pursuit of wisdom, and in the work he has to do. This enjoyment, he says, comes as a gift of God (2:24-26). But beneath the account of all these efforts, the pedal note drones on: *"hevel, hevel,* all is *hevel"* (1:14; 2:1, 11, 15, 17, 19, 21, 23, 26).

Ecclesiastes 3 and 4

Now the author begins to focus on some of life's problems, as he sees them. He begins to talk about God, to talk theology. There are times for all things in life, he says, and God has set these times (3:1-8). But we humans have certain problems: (1) No matter how hard we try, we can't figure out what God is up to (3:11). (2) As we look about us, we see that the world is full of wickedness and injustice (3:16; 4:1-3). (3) Like all creatures, we eventually die, and we don't really know what death means for any of us (3:18-21) , though we do know that we can't take our possessions with us into any next life (4:7-8)! So we are advised to accept God's gifts of friendship (3:12-13), joy in work (3:13, 22) and in community (4:7-12). But in the background, that organ note continues to sound: *"hevel, hevel,* all is *hevel"* (3:19; 4:4, 7, 8, 16).

Ecclesiastes 5

Ecclesiastes 4 had been concerned about earthly things. The focus was on matters "under the sun" — that is, things on this earth (4:1, 3, 7, 15), such as oppression and the place of work in human life (4:1-3, 7-8). Now the author begins to talk about heavenly things (5:2), about theology — that is, about God. Here for the first time in the book is some *instruction,* with verbs in the imperative mood. Humans are instructed to approach God's house carefully when going to worship. They are instructed to listen, to be careful with words, and to "fear God," to have respect and reverence for God (5:1-7).

In vv. 8-17 the Teacher returns to some earthly things ("under the sun," 5:13), offering comments on oppression and on the responsibilities that come to the wealthy.

The last section (5:18-20) again speaks of God (4 times) and gives advice for enjoying life on this earth ("under the sun," v. 18). The focus is again on table fellowship and on finding enjoyment in one's work and possessions, all understood as gifts of God. The chapter ends on a positive note, speaking of humans with joy in their hearts (5:20). But again in these reflections and observations, one can still hear that pedal note, "This also is *hevel*" (5:10; see v. 7).

Ecclesiastes 6–8

Ecclesiastes 6 begins by describing the sad situation of a person who had wealth and honor and a good life which was cut short by an early death. Behind the Teacher's report about this situation is a recommendation to "enjoy life's good things" (v. 3). An editorial note in the margin of the Hebrew Bible indicates that 6:9 marks the end of the first half of the book.

Ecclesiastes 6:10-12 introduces the second half of the book with a reminder of the brevity of human life and of the fact that humans do not know what their future will bring. The death theme introduced in 6:1-4 continues into chapter 7 with reminders of human mortality (7:1-13). The Teacher counsels enjoying life when such is possible, and offers a reminder of human ignorance about the future (7:14). That lamenting of the limits of human knowledge continues into chapter 8 (vv. 1, 7, 16-17), as does the call to enjoy life (v. 15). But in the background the pedal point, "This is *hevel*," continues to drone on (6:2, 4, 9, 11; 7:15; 8:10, 14 twice).

Ecclesiastes 9 and 10

At the beginning of chapter 9, the author strikes the *memento mori* (Latin "remember you must die") theme (9:1-6). Following this reminder, the Teacher offers a long section of *instruction* with imperative verbs, counseling the enjoyment of table fellowship, attractive clothing and pleasant fragrances, life with one's spouse, and daily work (9:7-10). Verses 11-12 describe the chanciness of human existence and verses 13-18 declare the superiority of wisdom over might. Chapter 10 collects some observations on life similar to those found in the book of Proverbs. Themes include a warning against excessive talking (vv. 12-14a; compare 5:2) and a reminder of the unknowability of the future (v. 14b; compare the comments on 3:11 above). The "enjoy the gifts God has given" theme occurs as instruction in 9:7-10, for once drowning out any striking of the *hevel* theme in these two chapters. One even hears the sounds of feasting and laughter in 10:19, reminiscent of Ps 104:15.

Ecclesiastes 11 and 12

The theme "you do not know" (see chapter 3) is expressed three times in 11:1-6 (vv. 2, 5, 6), declaring human ignorance in matters of natural disasters, the work of God, and agriculture. Ecclesiastes 11:7– 12:8 picks up themes typical of the Teacher, instructing senior citizens (11:8) but mainly young persons to enjoy each day and also to remember their Creator while life lasts. The *hevel* theme sounds in 11:8 and 10, and then three final times in 12:8, reaching back to 1:2.

An editor's epilogue offers a glance into the Teacher's workshop and then provides a brief summary of what the Teacher has been getting at in the book as a whole: "Fear God, and keep God's commandments" (12:9-13).

Luther on Ecclesiastes: ". . . so that we may happily enjoy . . ."

Luther gave a series of some 27 lectures on Ecclesiastes in Wittenberg, Germany, between July and November 1526. These lectures have been collected and edited by students and are now available as a part of volume 15 in *Luther's Works*. Following are some of the themes of Luther's approach to the book:

No *"Contempt of the World"*

In the Preface to the volume, Luther speaks of

> many of the saintly and illustrious theologians in the church, who
> thought that [in Ecclesiastes] Solomon was teaching what they call
> "the contempt of the world," that is, the contempt of things that
> have been created and established by God. Among these is St.
> Jerome, who by writing a commentary on this book urged Blesilla
> to accept the monastic life. From this source there arose and spread
> over the entire church, like a flood, that theology of the religious
> orders or monasteries. It was taught that to be a Christian meant to
> forsake the household, the political order . . . to flee to the desert, to
> isolate oneself from human society, to live in stillness and silence;
> for it was impossible to serve God in the world. (p. 4)

Against this background, Luther gave his own lectures on Ecclesiastes, which took a much different approach to that book.

Living in the Midst of the World

Luther believed that it was not necessary to flee the world in order to
serve God. In fact, according to Ecclesiastes, one ought to serve God
in the midst of the world! Luther writes in regard to Eccl 7:1-2: "But
Christians should be exhorted to live in the very midst of the crowd,
to marry, to govern their household, etc. Moreover, when their efforts are hindered by the malice of men, they should bear it patiently
and not cease their good works. Do not desert the battlefield but
stick it out" (p. 106).

The book of Ecclesiastes could be of great help, Luther argued, to
those involved in public life: "But this book can give counsel to a
man involved in the state or the household as he deals with difficult
problems, and it can instruct and encourage his mind as he bears the
troubles of such a position." In fact, says Luther, "unless there is
some Solomon to exhort and console him, government crushes the
man, extinguishes him, and utterly destroys him" (p. 5).

The Purpose of the Book of Ecclesiastes

Of special interest and value are the suggestions Luther makes about how to go about interpreting the book of Ecclesiastes. The parts, he says, should be understood in the light of the purpose of the whole book. Luther states that purpose in several contexts. At the beginning of the lectures he says:

> The summary and aim of this book, then, is as follows: Solomon wants to put us at peace and to give us a quiet mind in the everyday affairs and business of this life, so that we live contentedly in the present without care and yearning about the future and are, as Paul says, without care and anxiety (Phil 4:6). It is useless to plague oneself with anxiety about the future. (p. 7)

Ecclesiastes 2:24 is the first of the passages in the book that counsel enjoyment: "There is nothing better for mortals than to eat and drink, and find enjoyment in their toil. This also, I saw, is from the hand of God." Commenting on this verse, Luther says: "This is the principal conclusion, in fact the point, of the whole book, which he will often repeat. This is a remarkable passage, one that explains everything preceding and following it" (p. 46). Luther again sounds what he considers to be the theme of the entire book, in his exposition of 5:20, which reads:

"For they will scarcely brood over the days of their lives, because God keeps them occupied with the joy of their hearts." Comments Luther: "This is the conclusion of this entire book or argument. . . . This statement is the interpreter of the entire book: Solomon intends to forbid vain anxieties, so that we may happily enjoy the things that are present and not care at all about the things that are in the future, lest we permit the present moment, our moment, to slip away" (p. 93).

Summary

While Ecclesiastes has often not been appreciated in biblical scholarship and has been neglected in the churches, there is a new interest in that book today, especially in biblical scholarship. The thematic word of the book is *hevel,* traditionally translated as "vanity," and that word continues to sound throughout the entire book, like a sustained pedal point on an organ.

Luther understands Ecclesiastes not as a summons to flee the things of the world, but as a call to worldly involvement. In Luther's view, Ecclesiastes can be of special value precisely to those involved in the running of the state or of the household. Each section of Ecclesiastes should be read in the light of the purpose of the book as a whole. That purpose, according to Luther, is to drive away anxiety and worry and to encourage a life of happiness, enjoying the things that are present as God's gifts, being involved in the activities of public life, and not worrying about what may come in the future.

We shall keep listening for that pedal point and shall keep Luther's interpretive suggestions before us as we continue to read through Ecclesiastes.

2 Is That All There Is?
Ecclesiastes 1–2

So, the woman who dreamed of marrying a successful doctor or corporate exec-utive and living in a fancy house in the suburbs may find herself well married and living in her dream house but cannot understand why she goes around ev-ery morning saying to herself, "Is this all there is to life?"

Harold Kushner, *When All You've Ever Wanted Isn't Enough*, pp. 17-18

Is that all there is? Is that all there is? If that's all there is, my friends, then let's keep dancing.

Song by Jerry Leiber and Mike Stoller, recorded by Peggy Lee

Let us, therefore, be content with the things that are present and commit our-selves into the hand of God, who alone knows and controls both the past and the future.

Martin Luther, *Notes on Ecclesiastes*, p. 10

The melody is simple, easily hummable, composed by the songwriting team that also gave the world Elvis Presley's

"Hound Dog." The lyrics are haunting, expressing disillusionment, but calling for life to be enjoyed, nevertheless. The recording won a Grammy Award in 1970 for "Best Contemporary Vocal Performance, Female." The singer was Norma Deloris Egstrom of Jamestown, North Dakota, better known as Miss Peggy Lee.

The search and the sentiments expressed in this song are reminiscent of the search and sentiments expressed in the opening chapters of the biblical book of Ecclesiastes. The song alternates words spoken with words sung as a refrain:

> (spoken) I remember when I was a very little girl, our house caught on fire. I'll never forget the look on my father's face as he gathered me up in his arms and raced through the burning building out to the pavement. I stood there shivering in my pajamas and watched the whole world go up in flames. And when it was all over I said to myself, "Is that all there is to a fire?"

> (refrain) Is that all there is? Is that all there is?
> If that's all there is, my friends, then let's keep dancing.
> Let's break out the booze and have a ball, if that's all there is.

> (spoken) And when I was 12 years old, my father took me to a circus, the greatest show on earth. There were clowns and elephants and dancing bears, and a beautiful lady in pink tights flew high above our heads. And so I sat there watching the marvelous spectacle. I had the feeling that something was missing. I didn't know what, but when it was over, I said to myself, "Is that all there is to a circus?"

> (refrain) Is that all there is . . . ?

> (spoken) Then I fell in love, head over heels, with the most wonderful boy in the world. We would take long walks by the river or just sit for hours gazing into each other's eyes. We were so very much in love. Then one day he went away and I thought I'd die, but I didn't. And when I didn't I said to myself, "Is that all there is to love?"

(refrain) Is that all there is . . . ?

(spoken) I know what you must be saying to yourselves. If that's the way she feels about it, why doesn't she just end it all? Oh no, not me. I'm in no hurry for that final disappointment. For I know just as well as I'm standing here talking to you, when that final moment comes and I'm breathing my last breath, I'll be saying to myself,

(sung) Is that all there is . . . ?[1]

More than three decades after the song was written and recorded, the background (possibly based on an essay by the German novelist Thomas Mann) and the meaning of the song continue to be discussed on the Internet. In any case, the song declares that the most exciting things that life has to offer — a housefire, a circus, a love affair — all end up being disappointing. And "if that is all there is," says the song's refrain, "then let's keep on dancing. . . . Let's enjoy what we can of life, while we can!"

When All You've Ever Wanted Isn't Enough

Rabbi Harold Kushner achieved literary fame with his best-seller dealing with the biblical book of Job, *When Bad Things Happen to Good People* (1981). Among his other publications is a study of Ecclesiastes, *When All You've Ever Wanted Isn't Enough: The Search for a Life That Matters* (1986). The woman Kushner quotes at the beginning of this chapter asks the same question that is asked in the song: "Is this all there is to life?" Kushner gives another example:

> I remember reading of a young man who left home to find fame and fortune in Hollywood. He had three dreams when he set out —

1. The song is available on a number of collections of Peggy Lee's music; e.g., Peggy Lee, *All-Time Greatest Hits, Volume 1,* Curb Records compact disk D2-77379.

to see his name in lights, to own a Rolls-Royce, and to marry a beauty contest winner. By the time he was thirty, he had done all three, and he was a deeply distressed young man, unable to work creatively anymore despite (or perhaps because of) the fact that all of his dreams had come true. By thirty, he had run out of goals. What was there for him to do with the rest of his life? (p. 17)

This young man had achieved much but was still dissatisfied and distressed. We could imagine him, in a reflective moment, asking, "Is this all there is?" This young man and the woman mentioned above are in the same boat. Both are disillusioned and disappointed. They are illustrations of an observation by psychologist Carl Jung: "About a third of my cases are suffering from no clinically definable neurosis, but from the senselessness and emptiness of their lives. This can be described as the general neurosis of our time" (Kushner, p. 18).

The Hebrew word *hevel,* traditionally translated as "vanity," could also be translated, using Jung's words, "senselessness and emptiness." Ecclesiastes is well acquainted with the ailment that Jung identified as "the general neurosis of our time."

The introduction to Ecclesiastes in 1:1-2, which sounds the theme (the "pedal point") for the entire book, has been discussed in the previous chapter. We turn now to consider the argument of the Teacher, Qoheleth, in the remainder of these first two chapters of Ecclesiastes.

What Can Give My Life Meaning? (Ecclesiastes 1:3–2:23)

As Gerhard von Rad has observed, Qoheleth immediately goes after the big questions. And the first big question is about the meaning of life itself. In these first two chapters, Qoheleth tests three possible answers to questions like those raised by Peggy Lee's song or by Kushner's bored businessman or tired housewife. At issue in each of these cases is the question: What can give meaning to my life?

What about Work? (1:3-11)

3 What do people gain from all the toil
   at which they toil under the sun?
4 A generation goes, and a generation comes,
   but the earth remains forever.
5 The sun rises and the sun goes down,
   and hurries to the place where it rises.
6 The wind blows to the south,
   and goes around to the north;
 round and round goes the wind,
   and on its circuits the wind returns.
7 All streams run to the sea,
   but the sea is not full;
 to the place where the streams flow,
   there they continue to flow.
8 All things are wearisome;
   more than one can express;
 the eye is not satisfied with seeing,
   or the ear filled with hearing.
9 What has been is what will be,
   and what has been done is what will be done;
 there is nothing new under the sun.
10 Is there a thing of which it is said,
   "See, this is new"?
 It has already been,
   in the ages before us.
11 The people of long ago are not remembered,
   nor will there be any remembrance
 of people yet to come
   by those who come after them.

For many persons, what gives meaning to their lives is their work. Our age has coined the word "workaholic," which refers to people who do not just work to live but who live to work (see Chapter 4 below).

Qoheleth states his main point in verse 3 in the form of a question; the expression "under the sun" means "here on this earth" and is so translated in the Contemporary English Version (CEV): "What is there to show for all of our hard work here on this earth?" The implied answer is, "Nothing at all!" The same matter comes up when the author asks, "What gain have the workers from all their toil?" in 3:9 (also 5:16). "You work and work for years and years, you're always on the go" — but you have nothing to show for it, Qoheleth is saying, in the words of the old song ("Enjoy Yourself, It's Later than You Think"). The author summarizes: "Then I considered all that my hands had done and the toil I had spent in doing it, and again, all was vanity and a chasing after wind, and there was nothing to be gained under the sun" (2:11). In Qoheleth's view, it appears as if all the work being done by humans is nothing but plodding along on a gigantic treadmill, accomplishing nothing, going nowhere (1:4-7). Says the author, "All of life is far more boring than words could ever say" (v. 8 CEV).

Qoheleth appears to be bored and never satisfied. Life is just "the same old, same old," one same old thing after another (vv. 9-11). And work? It's like the song from *Porgy and Bess* puts it: "Ah gits weary an' sick of tryin', Ah'm tired of livin' and sceered of dyin'." Work can be back-breaking or mind-aching, with plenty of pain but not much gain. Meanwhile, says Qoheleth, the sun rises and sets, the wind blows to the south and comes around again in the north, all streams flow to the sea, or as the song puts it, "Ol' Man River, he jus' keeps rollin' along."

So what can give life a sense of purpose and meaning? That is Qoheleth's question, and it can be the question for 21st-century people as well. If work can't give my life meaning, then what about wisdom? If labor doesn't bring a sense of satisfaction, then what about learning?

What about Education? (1:12-18)

12I, the Teacher, when king over Israel in Jerusalem, 13applied my mind to seek and to search out by wisdom all that is done under heaven; it is an unhappy business that God has given to human beings to be busy with. ¹⁴I saw all the deeds that are done under the sun; and see, all is vanity and a chasing after wind.

15   What is crooked cannot be made straight,
         and what is lacking cannot be counted.

¹⁶I said to myself, "I have acquired great wisdom, surpassing all who were over Jerusalem before me; and my mind has had great experience of wisdom and knowledge." ¹⁷And I applied my mind to know wisdom and to know madness and folly. I perceived that this also is but a chasing after wind.

18   For in much wisdom is much vexation,
         and those who increase knowledge increase sorrow.

I recall a farm couple bringing their son to enroll as a freshman in the college where I was teaching. We were visiting in my office. They had been saving money for this day for years, they said. The wife told me that in addition to helping with the normal chores on the farm, she was working long hours each night in the local hatchery, candling eggs, to earn a few more dollars for tuition costs — all so that their son could get a college education. It was learning, education, they were sure, that would give their son's life meaning and purpose.

And I remember a boy in junior high school delivering newspapers and putting aside a dollar a week in the local savings and loan, watching the account grow, so that one day he could go to college. "Get a college education," his parents said. "Nobody can ever take that away from you!" Getting an education remains a central goal in our time. And education, or what the Bible calls "wisdom," is of central importance in the book of Ecclesiastes. In chapter 1, the word occurs in verses 13, 16 (twice), 17 and 18.

The author speaks of himself as being "king over Jerusalem." We have already noted that the writer of Ecclesiastes imagines himself as "king of Jerusalem" as a literary device.

Roland Murphy has observed that there are two similarly structured parts to this section: (1) verses 12-14 plus a supporting proverb in verse 15; and (2) verses 16-17 plus a supporting proverb in verse 18

(*Wisdom Literature,* p. 134). Here the Teacher is engaging in role play, imagining himself as King Solomon, remembered as the wisest king ever to rule over Israel (1 Kgs 4:29-34). This Teacher, Qoheleth, is telling us that he had thrown himself into his studies with dedication and passion. But as he looks back on those years of hitting the books and sitting at the feet of the masters, it now seems to him that all this intellectual effort had led only to unhappiness. Looking back, it all seems to be have been *hevel,* a puff of smoke, not lasting, a waste of time and effort (v. 14; see also the teacher's observation in 12:12b, "much study is a weariness of the flesh").

Verses 16 and 17 make the same point again. Still assuming the role of King Solomon, Qoheleth reports having achieved great intellectual accomplishments. He had achieved an international reputation as a scholar (see 1 Kings 4:29-31)! But he finally decides that it has not been worth it. The TEV translation makes it crystal clear: "The wiser you are, the more worries you have; the more you know, the more it hurts" (v. 18).

Let us bring the matter up to our own time. We could imagine a bright college student who discovers the joys of intellectual accomplishment and even becomes the valedictorian of his senior class. His professors encourage him to continue his studies, and he wins a Rhodes Scholarship and spends two wonderful years studying further in Oxford, England! He continues his education at Harvard, by this time with a wife and a couple of children to cheer him on. Soon he has an M.A., then a Ph.D., and is awarded a position as a junior professor at Stanford. His list of publications grows, his speaking invitations multiply, and he has become an authority in his field. He installs a cot in his office so that he can camp out there during the week, get an earlier start on his research and writing each day, and save on commuting time. But then late one night, as he sits at his desk, his head aching from too much coffee and not enough sleeping, he glances up at the diplomas and awards on his wall and notices the pictures of his wife and children on his desk. He realizes that he is at the top of his academic heap, but he is not happy. He asks, "Has it all been worth it?" He mentally paraphrases an old hymn he learned as a child: What will it mean "if I gain the world, but lose my family"? What if I win a Guggenheim but don't get to know my girls? What if I'm awarded a Nobel prize but lose my soul? What started as an invigorating pursuit of a Ph.D. is now coming close to an exhausting breakdown. "For in much wisdom is much vexation," is the way Qoheleth puts it.

What can give my life purpose and meaning? That has been the question. And the quest continues. The Teacher tells us more about it.

Or Why Not Live for Pleasure?
Will That Satisfy My Longing? *(2:1-11)*

¹I said to myself, "Come now, I will make a test of pleasure; enjoy yourself." But again, this also was vanity. ²I said of laughter, "It is mad," and of pleasure, "What use is it?" ³I searched with my mind how to cheer my body with wine — my mind still guiding me with wisdom — and how to lay hold on folly, until I might see what was good for mortals to do under heaven during the few days of their life. ⁴I made great works; I built houses and planted vineyards for myself; ⁵I made myself gardens and parks, and planted in them all kinds of fruit trees. I made myself pools from which to water the forest of growing trees. ⁷I bought male and female slaves, and had slaves who were born in my house; I also had great possessions of herds and flocks, more than any who had been before me in Jerusalem. ⁸I also gathered for myself silver and gold and the treasure of kings and of the provinces; I got singers, both men and women, and delights of the flesh, and many concubines.

⁹So I became great and surpassed all who were before me in Jerusalem; also my wisdom remained with me. ¹⁰Whatever my eyes desired I did not keep from them; I kept my heart from no pleasure, for my heart found pleasure in all my toil, and this was my reward for all my toil. ¹¹Then I considered all that my hands had done and the toil I had spent in doing it, and again, all was vanity and a chasing after wind, and there was nothing to be gained under the sun.

The search goes on. If neither work nor intellectual accomplishment will give meaning to life, then what about pleasure? Why not live for sheer pleasure? The word "pleasure" occurs four times in this short section (vv. 1 and 2, twice in v. 10). The result of this experiment in pleasure is already given in verses 1 and 2: the efforts to find enjoyment will finally end up as *hevel* (v. 1), and Qoheleth says of pleasure, "What use is it?" But now the writer tells us more about the "pleasure hunt" phase of his quest for meaning.

Verses 3-10 offer a recital of the things the Teacher has accomplished. He has become an expert in wines and can speak intelligently about the body, the bouquet, the flavor of the great variety of wines available in the Mediterranean world (v. 3; note also what is said about the delights of wine in 9:7!). At the center of concern in this recital is the self. Notice words like "I" or "my" or "myself." In the Hebrew, "for me" occurs 13 times in these few verses!

Can we imagine this quester in our own world? According to *Food and Wine* magazine, he has become one of the great gourmands of his day. *Vanity Fair* reports that one of the most coveted invitations in the city is an evening in the penthouse that he and his wife share. The walls of their living room feature originals by Jackson Pollock, Robert Rauschenburg, and Jasper Johns. A *New Yorker* columnist has suggested that our quester out-trumps Donald Trump!

Back to the biblical text. We may observe that the pleasures Qoheleth was sampling were not only those sensual ones of the "eat, drink, and be merry" sort. Verses 4-6 tell of more sophisticated satisfactions. He reports of having conceived, designed, and completed a variety of building projects. *Architectural Digest* might have named him "designer of the year." He shows his guests around his property. They marvel at the houses and gardens, the vineyards and parks, the orchards with exotic fruit trees and highly technical irrigation systems. Qoheleth tells about his cadre of workers and servants and reports that on his staff now are children of servants born while their parents were in his employ! He speaks of being engaged in ranching, raising sheep and other animals. In our time, he would no doubt have had a stable of sleek polo ponies! In fact, he had more possessions than anyone ever had before him (v. 7)! Finally, he tells of great wealth and extensive treasures, of both male and female staff musicians, and he lets us know that "I had all the women a man could want" (v. 8 TEV). Verse 10 wraps it up. "Pleasure" is emphasized with two occurrences: "I kept my heart from no pleasure, for my heart found pleasure in all my toil." He has been a self-made man. No doubt he had stories about taking on hard tasks as a boy, developing a crew of workers, getting more and more contracts, and finally becoming president of his own company!

The Teacher had built a magnificent residence, an international reputation, and led a style of life worthy of the rich and famous. We might suggest that he was Bill Gates, Tom Cruise, and Hugh Hefner, all rolled into one. He enjoyed fine music, plenty of money, plenty of sex, the best food, the most exotic wines (v. 8). And he can sit back and say, not without a good deal of pride, "I've earned it all with these two hands!"

But verse 11 indicates that there is something hollow and unsatisfying about all this. As he sits alone, late at night, reaching for another glass of brandy and reflecting on his life and work, he concludes that it has all added up to *hevel*, nothingness, as substantial and lasting as a cloud of vapor or a puff of steam or a wisp of smoke. The Hebrew text lines up two sets of alliteration, saying *"hinneh, hakol, hevel,"* "behold, it was all worthless and temporary," and *"re˓ut ruach,"* "a chasing after the wind." To try to hold onto this playboy lifestyle, with its wealth and its pleasures, would be like trying to capture the wind or to fence in the breeze. The Teacher had all that he had ever wanted. But it wasn't enough. And so the Teacher tells us more.

One More Time: Education and Work (2:12-23)

¹²So I turned to consider wisdom and madness and folly; for what can the one do who comes after the king? Only what has already been done. ¹³Then I saw that wisdom excels folly as light excels darkness.

14   The wise have eyes in their head,
         but fools walk in darkness.

Yet I perceived that the same fate befalls all of them. ¹⁵Then I said to myself, "What happens to the fool will happen to me also; why then have I been so very wise?" And I said to myself that this also is vanity. ¹⁶For there is no enduring remembrance of the wise or of fools, seeing that in the days to come all will have been long forgotten. How can the wise die just like fools? ¹⁷So I hated life, because what is done under the sun was grievous to me; for all is vanity and a chasing after wind.

¹⁸I hated all my toil in which I had toiled under the sun, seeing that I must leave it to those who come after me ¹⁹and who knows whether they will be wise or foolish? Yet they will be master of all for which I toiled and used my wisdom under the sun. This also is vanity. ²⁰So I turned and gave my heart up to despair concerning all the toil of my labors under the sun, ²¹because sometimes one who has toiled with wisdom and knowledge and skill must leave all to be enjoyed by another who did not toil for it. This also is vanity and a great evil. ²²What do mortals get from all the toil and strain with which they toil under the sun? ²³For all their days are full of pain, and their work is a vexation; even at night their minds do not rest. This also is vanity.

Qoheleth is a teacher. Like all teachers, he knows that repetition is the key to learning. And so he goes over these three proposed answers to the question of life's meaning, one more time.

At first, his conclusions take on a negative tone. In reconsidering the value of education (vv. 12-17; see also 1:3-11), Qoheleth concludes that having learned something is at least better than being foolish: "Wisdom is like having two good eyes; foolishness leaves you in the dark" (2:13 CEV). But both the wise and the foolish will die (v. 16). His conclusion sounds dangerously depressed: "So I hated life" (v. 17).

Then Qoheleth takes another look at work as life's ultimate concern, in verses 18-23 (see also 1:12-18). His discussion is focused and hard-hitting. The word "toil" (nicely translated as "hard work" in

CEV) occurs seven times in this short section. With verse 18 he picks up "I hated" from 2:17 and gives three reasons why he hates his work: (1) He can't take it with him (vv. 18-19)! (2) He knows he'll have to leave it all to someone who hasn't worked for it (vv. 20-21)! (3) It's been too much strain without much gain, and too often worry about work has robbed him of a good night's sleep (vv. 22-23; see also 8:16-17)!

Living for work, for learning, or for pleasure have all ended up in disappointment. Each has left the Teacher saying, "Is this all there is?" So what advice does he now have for his young (see 12:1) students?

So Enjoy! (Ecclesiastes 2:24-26)

24There is nothing better for mortals than to eat and drink, and find enjoyment in their toil. This also, I saw, is from the hand of God; 25for apart from him who can eat or who can have enjoyment? 26For to the one who pleases him God gives wisdom and knowledge and joy; but to the sinner he gives the work of gathering and heaping, only to give to one who pleases God. This also is vanity and a chasing after wind.

After the gloominess of chapters 1 and 2 to this point, the mood now changes, with this first sounding of the "enjoy life" theme in the book of Ecclesiastes (2:24-26). Now Qoheleth has a positive recommendation, saying "Listen up! There is nothing better than this!" And here he commends the joy of being together with friends at table and the enjoyment to be found in doing meaningful work. Then he makes a statement about God — in other words, a theological observation: these things, eating and drinking together with family and friends, bring us into contact with God! And notice that here is joy *in* work, not just joy *in the results* of work! In fact, good times with friends, days filled with meaningful and enjoyable work — these are the best things in life, and they are God's gifts, elsewhere named God's blessings.

33

We pause for a moment to ask about the Teacher's understanding of God. We shall see that, while Qoheleth does believe in God, he has what may be described as a major theological problem. God seems very far away, and humans cannot figure out what God is doing (see Chapter 5 below). Here in 2:24-26, however, is a hint indicating how God spans the gap between heaven and human beings. The gulf between God and humans is bridged in these instances that speak of humans receiving and enjoying God's gifts (see also 3:12-13; 3:22; 5:18-20; 8:15; 9:7-10; 11:8–12:1).

Other biblical references also point to the joys of table fellowship (e.g., Psalm 133) and in fact identify the Lord's table as the place where the gap between humans and God is overcome, in a joyful eating and drinking together (Matt. 8:11; 11:18-19; 22:1-4; Luke 15:1-2). The gulf between God and humans is bridged from God's side by God's giving of everyday good gifts.

The request "give us this day our daily bread" in the Lord's Prayer asks God to give the ordinary gifts that sustain human life. What is meant by this "daily bread"? The answer in Luther's Catechism points to these ordinary good things:

What then does "daily bread" mean?

Answer: Everything our bodies need such as food, drink, clothing, shoes, house, home, fields, livestock, money, property, an upright spouse, upright children, upright members of the household, upright and faithful rulers, good government, good weather, peace, health, decency, honor, good friends, faithful neighbors, and the like. (*Luther's Small Catechism*, p. 36)

Such are the ordinary gifts that God gives. The Bible names these God's "blessings." The Teacher, for all his criticism of most human activities and ventures, says that there is nothing better for human beings than to enjoy these ordinary gifts.

In summary, still sounding beneath the whole discussion in these chapters has been that sustained bass note, that pedal point, *"hevel,*

hevel," "all is vanity, a vapor, meaningless" (1:2, 14; 2:1, 11, 17, 19, 21, 23, 26). But now another more upbeat, brighter theme has been introduced in counterpoint against that sustained bass: the theme of finding *joy* in life together with others and even in one's daily work (2:24-26). We shall continue to hear this ode to joy in the discussions that follow (3:12-13, 22; 5:18-20; 8:15; 9:7-10; 11:8-10) and shall focus on it in Chapter 7 below. In any case, we begin to sense that Qoheleth is catching a hint of an answer to the reasons for his perpetual dissatisfactions, and to his restless questions about the meaning of life and about God.

3 Who Knows?
Ecclesiastes 3

To everything — turn, turn, turn,
  there is a season — turn, turn, turn,
and a time for every purpose under heaven.

Song by Pete Seeger (1954)[1]

Who knows? Who knows anyway? That's what I think about all this stuff!

College freshman, to this point in the required Bible
course bored and uninterested, coming alive and
interrupting my lecture, as I read Eccl 3:21

But, to put it plainly, for a man in his wife's arms to be hankering after the
other world is, in mild terms, a piece of bad taste, and not God's will. We ought
to find and love God in what he actually gives us; if it pleases him to allow us
to enjoy some overwhelming earthly happiness, we must not try to be more pi-
ous than God himself. . . . "For everything there is a season" (Eccles. 3:1).

Dietrich Bonhoeffer, *Letters and Papers*
from Prison, pp. 168-69

1. (New York: Melody Trails, 1962).

S urely the most well-known text from the biblical book of Ecclesiastes is this poem about the times in 3:1-8. It is quoted in speeches, painted on placards, sewn on wall hangings, and sung by folk singers. Among the most memorable settings for this text is the song by Pete Seeger, "Turn, Turn, Turn (To Everything There Is a Season)," written in 1954, made popular by The Byrds in the 1960s, and still heard today. The song begins with a refrain which picks up the theme of the poem by quoting Eccl 3:1 and continues with an adaptation of verses 1-8. The song became a theme song for those opposed to the involvement of the United States in Vietnam in the 1960s. The punch line comes at the very end, and is supplied with a word of commentary: Now is a time for peace, and "I swear it's not too late!"

This text from Ecclesiastes has had a way of reappearing in a variety of political contexts. At the signing of the Israel-PLO peace pact in 1993, Israeli Prime Minister Yitzhak Rabin's address concluded with a quotation from Eccl 3:8, stating that there was "A time to love, a time to hate, a time of war and a time of peace." Then the prime minister declared, "Ladies and gentlemen, the time for peace has come."[2] In October 2002, Senator Paul Wellstone of Minnesota, who had opposed U.S. military involvement in Iraq, was tragically killed in a plane accident. When former Vice President Walter Mondale accepted the nomination to run for Wellstone's Senate seat, Mondale ended his acceptance speech in Minneapolis with an adaptation of this text from Ecclesiastes 3: "The Scriptures say: 'To everything there is a season. A time to weep and a time to laugh, a time to mourn and a time to dance.' Fate has thrust upon us a double season. It is both a time to break down and a time to build up. My fellow Minnesotans, let us mourn together, but let us also together make the music of democracy."[3]

2. "The Bible in the News," compiled by Leonard Greenspoon, *Bible Review* 17/2 (2001): 11.

3. *Minneapolis Star Tribune,* 31 October 2001, p. A17.

Who Knows What Time It Is? (Ecclesiastes 3:1-8, 11, 17)

1 For everything there is a season, and a time for
  every matter under heaven:
2 a time to be born, and a time to die;
  a time to plant, and a time to pluck up what is planted;
3 a time to kill, and a time to heal;
  a time to break down, and a time to build up;
4 a time to weep, and a time to laugh;
  a time to mourn, and a time to dance;
5 a time to throw away stones, and a time to gather
  stones together;
  a time to embrace, and a time to refrain from embracing;
6 a time to seek, and a time to lose;
  a time to keep, and a time to throw away;
7 a time to tear, and a time to sew;
  a time to keep silence, and a time to speak;
8 a time to love, and a time to hate;
  a time for war, and a time for peace.

The thesis of this short piece is stated at the beginning: there is a right time for everything. The Teacher develops the thesis with 14 balancing pairs. The point is that there is an appropriate time for each of the activities listed in 3:1-8. Farmers know that there is a time for planting and for harvesting (v. 2). Verse 3 appears to refer to wartime and verse 4 to the happiness and the tears that mark the seasons of human lives. The sense of verse 5a is not immediately clear, but it is most naturally understood in reference to clearing fields for planting (see Isa 5:2). "A time to tear" in verse 7 is a reference to mourning customs, when garments are torn to indicate extreme grief (Gen 37:34; 2 Sam 3:31). One of the concerns of wisdom instruction was helping to determine when was a time to speak and when to keep silent (Prov 25:11, "A word fitly spoken is like apples of gold in a setting of silver"). After indicating that there is "a time to love and a time to hate," the last line of the poem reverses the order of the parallel to the love/hate line, so that the piece ends on a positive note: there is "a time for war, and a time for peace."

This listing of times offers a sampling of the events and moods that make up human lives. But Qoheleth, the writer, has noticed something problematic here. We humans cannot determine these times, nor can we control them. This is most evident in the first in the list. No one has anything to say about the time when he or she is born. It is God who determines these times. Says the Teacher:

> [11][God] has made everything suitable for its time; moreover he has put a sense of past and future into their minds, yet they cannot find out what God has done from the beginning to the end.

The CEV translation of verse 11 makes the problem even more clear: "God makes everything happen at the right time. Yet none of us can ever fully understand all that he has done, and he puts questions in our minds about the past and the future." God has set certain times for birth, for death, and for the ordinary occasions of a lifetime, the Teacher believes. But, to paraphrase the ominous words from the Houston space center, "Humans — we have a problem!" Says the Teacher, we humans can't figure out when those times are!

Qoheleth continues:

> [17]I said in my heart, God will judge the righteous and the wicked, for he has appointed a time for every matter, and for every work.

Again, in the CEV translation: "So I told myself that God has set a time and a place for everything." The challenge for humans is to determine the right time for actions such as those listed above. The wisdom teachers offer instruction about doing the right things at the right time: it's important to harvest the crops when they are ready (Prov 10:5)! Early morning is the wrong time to call your neighbor on the telephone (Prov 27:14). The right word at the right time can be a precious gift (Prov 25:11) but at other times, the best gift may be simply your presence (see Job 2:13).

To summarize: Ecclesiastes 3:1-8 indicates that there are appropriate times for the actions and the words that make up a person's life. God is the one who appoints these times. God has made everything "suitable" for its time. The Hebrew word translated "suitable" is *yapheh,* usually rendered "beautiful": "In all the land there were no women so *beautiful* as Job's daughters" (Job 42:15); "Now in all Israel there was no one to be praised so much for his *beauty* as Absalom" (2 Sam 14:25). The German Bible translates the sentence, *"[Gott] hat alles schön gemacht zu seiner Zeit,"* "God has made everything beautiful for its time." The sense is that there is a right time, a "beautiful" time, for each of these human activities. Then the question for each of us is: Who knows what time it is? Who knows when it is the right time for breaking down or building up? Or for speaking or keeping silent? Or for making war, or making love, or making peace? Qoheleth says: Only God knows the right times. God has "appointed a time for every matter, and for every work" (3:17). The frustration for humans is that God "never gives us the satisfaction of fully understanding what he does" (v. 11 TEV). In other words, part of our problem as human beings is that too often we just don't know what God is up to! Our question in regard to these matters is often, "Who knows?" And we discover that this question, or the idea which it expresses, comes up frequently in Ecclesiastes. In what follows we shall now look at some of those passages in the book, beginning with Ecclesiastes 3, where Qoheleth asks, "Who knows?" or the equivalent.

Who Knows about Death? (Ecclesiastes 3:18-21)

¹⁸I said in my heart with regard to human beings that God is testing them to show that they are but animals. ¹⁹For the fate of humans and the fate of animals is the same; as one dies, so dies the other. They all have the same breath, and humans have no advantage over the animals; for all is vanity. ²⁰All go to one place; all are from the dust, and all turn to dust again. ²¹*Who knows* whether the

human spirit goes upward and the spirit of animals goes downward to the earth? (emphasis mine)

Whenever I read this text, I think of a question raised by Julie, a
young woman in a required college religion course that I was teaching. The time was the early 1970s, and even in our relatively small
church-related school we were sensing the effects of the world-wide
student rebellion against the Vietnam War. Just after the first class
session in the fall, when I had gone through the syllabus and explained the course requirements, Julie was at my desk with some
questions. She was a small woman, clutching her notebook and text-
books, wearing the large round glasses that were the fashion of the
time.

She got right to the point: "Do we *have* to take religion?"

Now that question, which I'd had before, always irritated me a
bit. I straightened up to my full height, looked down at her, and said,
"Yes you *have* to take religion. That's not my idea, you know. It's a
college requirement."

"Can't I take Philosophy 101 instead?" she asked.

"No," I replied. "The courses are quite different."

A number of students began to gather around to listen in on our
conversation.

Inspired by this audience, I launched into a narrative about pio-
neer farmers who settled these prairies, who sacrificed to build
churches, and sacrificed even more to build this college. I mentioned
that if she didn't like the requirements here, she could transfer to the
state college 60 miles to the north.

But Julie stayed in the class. And she proceeded to get on my
nerves each class period. She made a point of reading the newspaper
or a book for another course during my lectures. I was in therapy each
lunch hour with my wife, asking her what I should do. "Just ignore
her," was my wife's advice. "She's just trying to get your attention!"

And she was succeeding in doing that. She continued with her
attention-getting devices. During one class session she lit up a ciga-
rette. It was a large class, she was sitting by a window, and I just let

her smoke away. She was bored by my lectures relating Genesis 1–11 to the world's environmental crisis. She had no interest in the Joseph story, even though it was accompanied by a recording of "Joseph and the Amazing Technicolor Dreamcoat." The section on Amos and social justice didn't interest her. And so on.

But then we came to Ecclesiastes. We discussed some of the options that have been suggested for thinking about God. We talked about atheism, the denial of the existence of God. We spoke of deism, which asserts that God exists but is not involved in the events of nature or history. We mentioned polytheism which proposes that there are many gods. Finally, I said some things about agnosticism which simply declares "I don't know" in many matters of religion, including God's existence.

How should the view of the writer of Ecclesiastes be described? We followed the author's search for life's meaning. We noted that Qoheleth wasn't satisfied with making his work his ultimate concern, or education, or even pleasure. When we came to Ecclesiastes 3, I read the section from verses 18-21. In more than four decades of teaching, I have been interrupted in mid-lecture only twice. This time I was reading Eccl 3:19-21: "For the fate of humans and the fate of animals is the same; as one dies, so dies the other. . . . *Who knows* whether the human spirit goes upward and the spirit of animals goes downward to the earth?"

Suddenly Julie came alive. Without raising her hand, she blurted out, "Right on! Who knows? Who knows about any of this religion stuff? That's just what I believe! Who knows, anyway?"

I invited her to comment further, which she did.

Somehow, Ecclesiastes had gotten to her. She wrote an essay on the book. She began paying attention in class. She would come up to my desk after class, not with complaints, but with more questions. After she graduated, I got a letter or two from her, and she sent me a recording of Buffy Saint Marie songs, because she thought they had religious significance. Julie helped me understand Ecclesiastes, because that ancient book somehow understood her, and it spoke to her.

Several features of this section in 3:18-21 are especially interesting. Here is a statement that sounds quite modern, in our time of concern for all creatures of the planet. Here is an indication that humans and animals are part of the same family. In fact, humans are named "animals" (v. 18). Both humans and animals die (v. 19). They are both made of the same raw material, "the dust" (see also Gen 2:7, 19), and both return to the dust (v. 20). And as for the fate of each of them after death? The text gives a typical Qoheleth-like answer: "Who knows?" (3:21)

We shall give more attention to what Ecclesiastes has to say about death in Chapter 6 below. For now, we may note a few additional passages where the author expresses a view that we might label agnosticism, that is, "Who knows?"

Who Knows about the Future? (Ecclesiastes 3:11; 6:12; 7:14; 8:1-7, 16-17; 9:12; 10:14; 11:1-6)

A number of passages express a specific frustration that Qoheleth has: he does not know what the future will bring. The TEV translation catches that frustration in 3:11: "[God] has given us a desire to know the future, but never gives us the satisfaction of knowing fully what he does." Says the CEV, "Yet none of us can fully understand all that [God] has done, and he puts questions in our minds about the past and the future."

The reference in 6:12 is at the beginning of the second section of the book (see p. 86 below). Here is another one of the "who knows" passages:

> For *who knows* what is good for mortals while they live the few days of their vain life, which they pass like a shadow? For who can tell them what will be after them under the sun? (emphasis mine)

The first question in this verse, "For *who knows* what is good," does have an answer, or more accurately, several answers, in the section that follows in 7:1-14. "What is good?" asks 6:12, and 7:1-14 lists a dozen "good" things, or at least some things that are "better than" others.

Yet another "who knows?" section is introduced by 8:1, "And *who knows* the interpretation of a thing?" The theme continues in 8:6-7, with the focus again on human inability to know the future:

> 6For every matter has its time and its way, although the troubles of mortals lie heavy upon them. 7Indeed, they do not know what is to be, for who can tell them how it will be?

"No one can anticipate the future," says 9:12, comparing humans to fish or birds who are suddenly and without warning caught in a trap.

Finally, two passages lament the general inability of humans to fathom the ways of God. Even "those who are wise," that is, the teachers, the professors and pundits of Qoheleth's day, cannot succeed in understanding God:

> 8 16Whenever I tried to become wise and learn what goes on in the world, I realized that you could stay awake night and day 17and never be able to understand what God is doing. However hard you try, you will never find out. Wise men may claim to know, but they don't. (TEV)

"You do not know the work of God, who makes everything," says the Teacher in 11:5, comparing our lack of knowledge about God to a matter that we continue to debate in the 21st century: When does human life begin in the womb? When is a person a human being? At the moment of conception? After a period of weeks in the womb? Or at the moment when the umbilical cord is cut and the child functions independent of the mother? Says the Teacher: "Just as you do not know how the breath comes to the bones in the mother's womb, so you do not know the work of God, who makes everything."

Our knowledge is limited. No one knows this better than those who farm the land. Farmers are here advised to keep at their work of planting, even though they never know whether or not there will be a crop each year (11:6). Finally, 10:14 sums up the Teacher's view about the poverty of our knowledge about what is to come: "No one knows what is to happen, and who can tell anyone what the future holds?"

One Thing I Do Know (John 9; Ecclesiastes 3:12-14, 22)

I recall hearing a professor of New Testament lecture on the 9th chapter of John's Gospel. The professor remarked, as an aside, that the first person he wished to see, upon arriving in heaven, was the man whose story is told in that text. The story: Jesus was walking with some of his close friends when they saw a blind man alongside the road. This provoked some theoretical conversation about the causes of blindness. Then Jesus cut the conversation and did something. He spat on the ground, made some mud, and spread the mud on the man's eyes. He told the man to wash in a nearby pool, which he did, and the man came back seeing. Bystanders who had observed all this couldn't believe it. They began to ask each other and the man about the whole experience: "Is this the same person? Or is it someone else who looks like him?" They asked the man, "How were you healed? What? Mud and water from the pool? Come now! Who is this person who healed you? He must be a sinner because he healed you on the Sabbath day, and that's not allowed! Where is this fellow now?"

The investigation continued. They asked the man's parents about the healing. The parents said, "Ask our son himself! He's old enough to tell you!" And when these critics asked the man who had been healed about the one who had healed him, his ringing answer was unforgettable: "Whether he is a sinner or not, I don't know. One thing I do know. I used to be blind, and now I can see!" (John 9:25, my translation).

This answer came from a man who didn't know who this healer was, or where he had come from, or where he was now. He didn't have all the answers. But one thing he did know: he had been blind, and now he could see.

45

We have seen that the Teacher in Ecclesiastes does not claim to have all the answers, that *"who knows?"* is a theme that recurs through the book. Therefore, when the Teacher does say *"I know,"* we should do well to listen carefully. We should expect that the Teacher will not spew out any tired, pious cliches! So what *does* Qoheleth know? What is it that he *is* certain about? In contrast to his typical "Who knows?" running through the book, he says:

> 3 12*I know* that there is nothing better for [human beings] than to be happy and enjoy themselves as long as they live; 13moreover, it is God's gift that all should eat and drink and take pleasure in all their toil. 14*I know* that whatever God does endures forever; nothing can be added to it, nor anything taken from it; God has done this, so that all should stand in awe before him. 22So I saw that there is nothing better than that all should enjoy their work, for that is their lot; who can bring them to see what will be after them? (emphasis mine)

The story line of the book of Ecclesiastes up to this point is this: the Teacher concludes that neither work, nor education, nor pleasure can provide the answer to the quest for a meaningful life. Qoheleth acknowledges that there is a God who is in control of all things. But he also points to a great frustration: God is far distant, and there is no way of knowing what God is doing. He anticipates what the apostle would one day write: "For now we see in a mirror, dimly. . . . Now I know in part; then I shall understand fully" (1 Cor 13:12). In the meantime, the Teacher advises, the best thing for humans to do is to enjoy the gifts God has given them, such as the enjoyment of one another's company at table and enjoyment in their work. And they should have reverence for God (3:14 TEV). Companionship, good food and drink, the satisfaction that comes with doing good work — these are gifts from God, and in this way God bridges the gap between heaven and humans.

But now, what about that God? Ecclesiastes 3:9-15 is an intensely theological section: it mentions God six times, as Giver of gifts including work and fellowship at table (vv. 10, 13), as Maker of things beautiful (v. 11), as inscrutable Doer in history (vv. 11, 14), before whom humans ought to stand with reverence and awe (v. 14). Verses 17 and 18 add to this theological segment the notions of God as Judge and God as One who tests humans. Here are the makings of a theology, that is, some organized notions about God.

And now, after some thoughts about certain troubling earthly matters (Eccl 4), we shall hear more of what the Teacher says about the God of whom he speaks in 3:9-15 (Eccl 5). But we ought not forget: beneath all of this, like a pedal point on an organ, the *hevel* theme continues to sound (3:19).

Bonhoeffer and Ecclesiastes: ". . . to enjoy some overwhelming earthly happiness"

Dietrich Bonhoeffer (1906-1945) was a pastor and a professor in Germany who was executed because of his role in the plot to kill Adolf Hitler. In his various writings, especially *Life Together,* his somewhat fragmentary *Ethics,* and in the collection *Letters and Papers from Prison,* he makes reference to the book of Ecclesiastes.

Life Together

Life Together was written in September and October of 1938, growing out of Bonhoeffer's two-year experience as director of the Confessing Church's seminar in Finkenwalde. In the section entitled "The Day Together" he cites passages from Ecclesiastes that advise enjoying life, including reflections on mealtime as a time for refreshment and joy:

> The breaking of bread has a festive quality. In the midst of the working day given to us again and again, it is a reminder that God rested after God's work, and that the Sabbath is the meaning and the goal of the week with its toil. Our life is not only a great deal of trouble and hard work; it is also refreshment and joy in God's

goodness. We labor, but God nourishes and sustains us. There is a reason to celebrate. People should not eat the bread of anxious toil (Ps. 127:2). Rather, "eat your bread with enjoyment" (Eccles. 9:7), "so I commend enjoyment, for there is nothing better for people under the sun than to eat, and drink, and enjoy themselves" (Eccles. 8:15). But, of course, "apart from him, who can eat or who can have enjoyment?" (Eccles. 2:25). It is said of the seventy elders of Israel who climbed Mount Sinai with Moses and Aaron that "they beheld God, and they ate and drank" (Exod. 24:11). God will not tolerate the unfestive, joyless manner in which we eat our bread with sighs of groaning, with pompous, self-important busyness, or even with shame. Through the daily meal God is calling us to rejoice, to celebrate in the midst of our working day. (p. 73)

Ethics

Bonhoeffer was never able to finish his *Ethics.* After his execution in 1945, his friend Eberhard Bethge gathered Bonhoeffer's fragmentary materials, written in 1940-43, and edited and published them in 1949. In the section entitled "The Right to Bodily Life," Bonhoeffer cites a number of texts from Ecclesiastes:

And thus the bodiliness which is willed by God to be the form of existence of man is entitled to be called an end in itself. This does not exclude the fact that the body at the same time continues to be subordinated to a higher purpose. But what is important is that as one of the rights of bodily life its preservation is not only a means to an end but also an end in itself. It is in the joys of the body that it becomes apparent that the body is an end in itself within the natural life. If the body were only a means to an end man would have no right to bodily joys. . . . If the body is rightly to be regarded as end in itself, then there is a right to bodily joys, even though these are not necessarily subordinated to some higher purpose. It is inherent in the nature of joy itself that it is spoilt by any thought of purpose. . . . Within the natural life the joys of the body are reminders of the eternal joy which has been promised to men by God. If a man is deprived of the possibility of bodily joys through his body being used exclusively as a means to an end, this is an infringement of the original right of bodily life. "There is nothing better for a man, than that he should eat and drink, and that he should make his soul enjoy good in his labour. This also I saw, that it was from the hand of God" (Eccl. 2:24). "I know that there is no good in them, but for a man to rejoice, and to do good in his life" (Eccl. 3:12). "Eat thy bread with joy, and drink thy wine with a merry heart; for God now accepteth thy works . . . under the sun" (Eccl. 9:7ff.). "Rejoice, O young man, in thy youth; and let thy heart cheer thee in the days of thy youth, and walk in the ways of thine heart, and in the sight of thine eyes: but know thou, that for all these things God will bring thee into judgement" (Eccl. 11:9). "Who can eat gladly and have enjoyment without him?" (Eccl. 2:25).

Once again, Bonhoeffer cites passages from sections in Ecclesiastes that counsel enjoyment. Notice that humans are to find enjoyment *in* their work, not just in the *result* of their work (Eccl 2:24). Notice also that in enjoying food and table fellowship, humans are able to be in contact with God. These things are in fact gifts of God, and true enjoyment is not possible without God (2:25).

In a section entitled "The 'Ethical' and the 'Christian' as a Theme," Bonhoeffer has some criticisms of those he calls "the moralists," and again cites Ecclesiastes:

They assume that a man must continually be doing something decisive, fulfilling some higher purpose and discharging some ultimate duty. This represents a failure to understand that in historical human existence everything has its time (Eccl. 3), eating, drinking and sleeping as well as deliberate resolve and action, rest as well as work, purposelessness as well as the fulfillment of purpose, inclination as well as duty, play as well as earnest endeavour, joy as well as renunciation. Their presumptuous misjudgement of this creaturely existence leads either to the most mendacious hypocrisy

or else to madness. It turns the moralist into a dangerous tormen-
tor, tyrant and clown, a figure of tragi-comedy. (pp. 260-61)

The result of these words is a freeing, good news effect. Humans
are not expected at all times to be working, to be doing something
productive, or to be doing their duty. There are also times for eating,
drinking, sleeping, and playing! And humans should engage in
these activities without a guilty conscience, because so God has designed them.

Letters and Papers from Prison

In a letter written to Eberhard Bethge from Tegel prison on the 18th
of December, 1943, Bonhoeffer once again refers to one of the "enjoy"
passages in Ecclesiastes:

> I believe that we ought to love and trust God in our *lives,* and in all
> the good things that he sends us, that when the time comes (but
> not before!) we may go to him with love, trust, and joy. But, to put
> it plainly, for a man in his wife's arms to be hankering after the
> other world is, in mild terms, a piece of bad taste, and not God's
> will. We ought to find and love God in what he actually gives us; if
> it pleases him to allow us to enjoy some overwhelming earthly hap-
> piness, we must not try to be more pious than God himself and al-
> low our happiness to be corrupted by presumption and arrogance,
> and by unbridled religious fantasy which is never satisfied with
> what God gives. God will see to it that the man who finds him in
> his earthly happiness and thanks him for it does not lack reminder
> that earthly things are transient, that it is good for him to attune
> his heart to what is eternal, and that sooner or later there will be
> times when he can say in all sincerity, "I wish I were home." But ev-
> erything has its time, and the main thing is that we keep step with
> God, and do not keep pressing on a few steps ahead — nor keep
> dawdling a step behind. It's presumptuous to want to have every-
> thing at once — matrimonial bliss, the cross, and the heavenly Jeru-

salem, where they neither marry nor are given in marriage. "For everything there is a season" (Eccles. 3.1); everything has its time: "a time to weep, and a time to laugh; . . . a time to embrace, and a time to refrain from embracing; . . . a time to rend, and a time to sew . . . and God seeks again what is past." (pp. 168-69)

Here again is a reminder of the pleasures of earthly happiness and of joy to be found in the ordinary gifts that God gives. God intends times for laughing and embracing, as Ecclesiastes says, as well as for more intentional, goal-oriented pursuits. One is reminded of these words from the Talmud: "In the world to come, each of us will be called to account for all the good things God put on earth which we refused to enjoy."

In a letter Bonhoeffer wrote from prison shortly before Christmas in 1943, he reports his increasing appreciation of the Old Testament:

My thoughts and feelings seem to be getting more and more like those of the Old Testament, and in recent months I have been reading the Old Testament much more than the New. It is only when one knows the unutterability of the name of God that one can utter the name of Jesus Christ; it is only when one loves life and the earth so much that without them everything seems to be over that one may believe in the resurrection and a new world; it is only when one submits to God's law that one may speak of grace; and it is only when God's wrath and vengeance are hanging as grim realities over the heads of one's enemies that something of what it means to forgive them can touch our hearts. In my opinion it is not Christian to want to take our thoughts and feelings too quickly and too directly from the New Testament. (pp. 156-57)

This developing appreciation for the Old Testament can be demonstrated from other parts of Bonhoeffer's writings as well. And, of course, these few quotations indicate that this appreciation included the book of Ecclesiastes.

In sum, then, we notice that Bonhoeffer took seriously what he discovered in Ecclesiastes. The passages he focuses on here are those that speak of the joy and delight of such earthly good things as food, fellowship, and love between a man and a woman. These ordinary good things are identified as gifts of God, or blessings. When such things come our way, advises Bonhoeffer, we should receive them with gratitude and with joy.[4]

4. See Gail Nord Paulson, "The Use of Qoheleth in Bonhoeffer's *Ethics*," *Word and World* 18 (1998): 307-13. For a complete listing of references to Ecclesiastes in the German edition of Bonhoeffer's works, see *Register und Ergänzungen: Dietrich Bonhoeffer Werke* 17, edited by Herbert Anzinger and Hans Pfeifer et al. (Gütersloh: Chr. Kaiser, 1999), pp. 280-81.

4 "Who's Been Working the Hardest?"
Ecclesiastes 4

Who's been working the hardest?

> Company president, the day after the funeral, inquiring about
> a replacement for the deceased (Ellen Goodman column)

One thing I've learned in the months since I've been here. In South Dakota, the
three cardinal sins are drinking, dancing, and sitting down.

> Inaugural speech of a newly elected college academic dean,
> after having moved from the East into the Midwest

In my years as a rabbi, I've visited many people lying on their death beds. But I
have yet to hear one say, "I wish I would have spent more time on my business."

> Harold Kushner, in a lecture given
> at Temple of Aaron, St. Paul

We have seen that chapter 3 of Ecclesiastes has a good deal to
say about God. The poem about the "seasons" in 3:1-8 indicates that these various times are in God's hands (v. 17) and human

beings cannot determine them (v. 11). The remainder of the chapter (vv. 9-22) reports a variety of God's actions, all in relationship to humans: God gives, makes, does, seeks, judges, and tests.

In Ecclesiastes 4, however, there is no mention of God at all. The focus of this chapter is upon things "under the sun" (vv. 1, 3, 7, 15), that is, upon things "on the earth." The chapter deals with such down-to-earth matters as the oppression of the powerless, the place of work in human life, the power of envy, the advantages of life together with others, and the temptations and dangers that come to political leaders. Ecclesiastes 4 is focused on earthly things; in contrast, chapter 5 will be concerned with heavenly things (Eccl 5:2), including God (mentioned 10 times).

It is instructive to note the types of sayings gathered in this chapter. There are three *reflections* of the Teacher, each introduced by "I saw . . ." (4:1-3, 4-6, 7-8):

> Again *I saw* all the oppressions that are practiced under the sun. (4:1)

> Then *I saw* that all toil and all skill in work . . . (4:4)

> Again *I saw* vanity under the sun. (4:7)

The chapter also includes four *better than* sayings. Such sayings are scattered throughout the Bible:

> Surely, to obey is *better* than sacrifice. (1 Sam 15:22)

> ". . . for I am no *better than* my ancestors." (1 Kgs 19:4)

> It is *better* to take refuge in the LORD
>   *than* to put confidence in mortals.
>
> (Ps 118:8; also v. 9)

They are typical of the Bible's Wisdom literature:

54

Better is a little with the fear of the LORD
   than great treasure and trouble with it.
Better is a dinner of vegetables where love is
   than a fatted ox and hatred with it.
                 (Prov 15:16-17; also 16:19, 32; 25:7; etc.)

These sayings occur frequently in Ecclesiastes (see 7:1, 2, 3, 5, 8, 10 and the discussion in Chapter 6 below). Two of these sayings in Ecclesiastes 4 are at the conclusion of *reflections,* introduced by "I saw":

Again I saw all the oppressions that are practiced under the sun. . . . And I thought the dead, who have already died, more fortunate than the living, who are still alive, but *better than* both is the one who has not yet been. (4:1-3)

Then I saw that all toil and all skill come from one person's envy
   of another. . . .
Better is a handful with quiet
   than two handfuls with toil.

                                 (4:4-6)

Two of them introduce independent sayings:

Two are *better than* one. (4:9)

Better is a poor but wise youth *than* an old but foolish king. (4:13)

All the Injustice (Ecclesiastes 4:1-3)

[1]Then I looked again at all the injustice that goes on in this world. The oppressed were crying, and no one would help them. No one would help them, because their oppressors had power on their side. [2]I envy those who are dead and gone; they are better off than those who are still alive. [3]But better off than either are those who

have never been born, who have never seen the injustice that goes
on in this world. (TEV)

This passage provides a rare insight into the Teacher's heart.
Qoheleth considers the world around him and is struck by the unfairness of it all. He identifies two classes of people: the oppressed
and the oppressors or, to use other terms, the powerless, who have
no one to help them, and the powerful, who use their considerable
resources and influence to oppress those without power. The
Teacher has noticed the tears in the eyes of the oppressed (4:1). The
repeated expression in verse 1, "no one would help them," provides
the clue for the concern of this section. The NRSV translates the
phrase, "with no one to comfort them." These persons are hurting
and are lonely. The same expression occurs in the sad poems
mourning the fall of Jerusalem that are gathered in the book of
Lamentations. Speaking of the fallen city as a lonely widow, the author says, "She has no one to comfort her" (Lam 1:2 NRSV; see also
1:9, 17, 21).

We do not ordinarily think of social justice, specifically the oppression of the powerless by the powerful, as a concern in Ecclesiastes. But such concern is expressed here, and it is one of the central
themes of the Bible. The *oppress* vocabulary is the same as that used
by the prophets. Amos, in the 8th century B.C.E., speaks against the
wealthy women of Samaria "who *oppress* the poor, who crush the
needy" (Amos 4:1). In a sermon in the temple area in the 7th century,
Jeremiah calls upon the people of Judah to change their ways:

For if you truly amend your ways and your doings, if you truly act
justly one with another, if you do not *oppress* the alien, the orphan,
and the widow, or shed innocent blood in this place, and if you do
not go after other gods to your own hurt, then I will dwell with you
in this place. (Jer 7:5-7)

The theme continues through the prophets. Says Ezekiel, in the 6th
century:

The people of the land have practiced extortion and committed robbery; they have *oppressed* the poor and needy, and have extorted from the alien without redress. (Ezek 22:29)

And after the exile, in the late 6th century, Zechariah recalls the preaching of earlier prophets (Zech 7:7) and picks up the same theme:

Thus says the LORD of hosts: Render true judgments, show kindness and mercy to one another; do not *oppress* the widow, the orphan, the alien, or the poor; and do not devise evil in your hearts against one another. (Zech 7:9 10)

The same *oppress* vocabulary occurs in Proverbs, where mistreatment of the poor is equated with an insult to God:

Those who *oppress* the poor insult their Maker,
    but those who are kind to the needy honor him.

(Prov 14:31; see also 22:16; 28:3)

This concern for the powerless is certainly nothing new with Ecclesiastes. In fact, this is a theme that runs through the Bible, from the earliest parts of the Old Testament on into the Gospels and the Letters of the New Testament.[1] Note, for example, a word from the prophet Isaiah, who attacks the political leaders of his day because they were enacting legislation that was biased against three groups of people. The prophet pronounces a "Woe" upon them, which is to say he is announcing their funeral beforehand:

Woe to those who decree iniquitous decrees,
    and the writers who keep writing oppression,
to turn aside the needy from justice
    and to rob the poor of my people of their right,

---

1. For a discussion of these themes, see my book, *The Prophets and the Powerless.*

> that widows may be their spoil,
>> and that they may make the fatherless their prey!
>>> (Isa 10:1-2 RSV)

Those responsible for enacting legislation in the Judah of Isaiah's day had put laws into effect which oppressed the poor, the widow, and the orphan. These three groups have in common the fact that they have no power in society and are thus easily taken advantage of. The widow has no husband to protect her, the orphan has no parents, and the poor have no money. They were — and are — representative of the powerless in any society.

Concern for these powerless also runs through the legal materials of the Old Testament. The Book of the Covenant (Exod 20:22–23:33) adds another to the category of the powerless: the stranger, who has no friend to offer protection:

> You shall not wrong a stranger or oppress him, for you were strangers in the land of Egypt. You shall not afflict any widow or orphan. (Exod 22:21-22 RSV)

These oppressed and powerless persons are hurting in two ways. They hurt because of the circumstances of their lives. We can find them in our cities: the homeless, camped out on the sidewalks, huddled over the heating grates, holding up signs asking for help, begging for food and money. Or the fatherless, living in housing units with young mothers who struggle to keep healthy enough to hold a job and put food on the table. Or the hopeless, living on a reservation in South Dakota, seeing no way to get out of the cycle of alcoholism and drug use that cripples their family life.

They also hurt because they are lonely. They have no friends or family who will help them. In the words of 4:9-12, they have no one to pick them up when they fall, or to keep them warm when they are cold, or to protect them against robbery or an attack.

Observing these homeless, hopeless, hurting, lonely persons, sitting on the streets and the sidewalks of the city, Qoheleth makes some extreme statements. The Teacher says that the situation of those who are dead is better than that of these victims of the injustices of their world! This is strong language, the language of exaggeration. The Teacher is not counseling suicide as the solution to the problems of these hurting persons. He is not speaking of death in the future at all, but is referring to the situation of "those who have already passed away," who are presumably better off than these people of the streets, for they no longer have to endure the tragedies of life.[2] In an extremely pessimistic mood, the Teacher can even say that those who have never been born, who have never experienced these results of this social injustice, are better off!

Working Hard (Ecclesiastes 4:4-6)

> [4]I have also learned why people work so hard to succeed: it is because they envy the things their neighbors have. But it is useless [Hebrew *hevel*]. It is like chasing the wind. [5]They say that a man would be a fool to fold his hands and let himself starve to death. [6]Maybe so, but it is better to have only a little, with peace of mind, than to be busy all the time with both hands, trying to catch the wind. (TEV)

This bit of instruction and the next both concern the place of work in human life. Qoheleth has already said that it is possible to find joy in one's work and that such joy is a gift from God (2:24; 3:22). But he has also observed persons for whom work is a problem. Their lives are out of balance. Perhaps we have seen them, too. Maybe we recognize them all too well! These are persons who live to work rather than work to live. Here the Teacher identifies the engine that drives such workers. That engine is envy of the neighbor who has things that I wish I had. Maybe that neighbor drives a BMW convertible or lives in a house with three garages or cruises the lakes on a Hobie Cat

2. Choon-Leong Seow, *Ecclesiastes* (New York: Doubleday, 1997), p. 187.

sailboat. But these "things their neighbors have" do not have to be matcrial possessions. One may also envy another's life, or skill, or marriage, or reputation.

In the lecture by Rabbi Harold Kushner quoted above, he observed that in the first part of one's life the motivation that drives one's actions is *competition*. The student competes to earn "A" grades in every class, or to make the first team, or to win a violinist's chair in the Cleveland Orchestra. Such competition, said Kushner, can be good, and healthy. In the first part of our lives we need to find out what our talents are and what we are good at! But in the second part of our lives, after we have settled into our vocations, said the rabbi, the key motivation for our actions ought not be competition but *connection*. "In your 40s and beyond," said Kuschner, "you ought not be worrying about whether you are the best preacher in town or the fastest runner in your age bracket (Eccl 9:11!), or whether you have the most impressive house on the block. In the second part of your life, you ought to concentrate on *connections,* nurturing friendships, tending to family matters." Wise words, I have thought, and totally in the spirit of Qoheleth.

If verse 4 describes the person obsessed by work, verse 5 picks up the other extreme, the person who is not willing to work. William P. Brown is right on target in commenting: "As toil can be all-consuming, so idleness is self-cannibalizing."[3] Verse 6 then speaks of a proper balance of work and rest. Says the Teacher: scaling down, having fewer possessions, with a measure of peace and calm, is far better than owning twice as many things, coupled with more worries and a frantic lifestyle!

The Lonely Workaholic (Ecclesiastes 4:7-8)

> [7]I have noticed something else in the world that is useless *[hevel]*.
> [8]Here is a man who lives alone. He has no son, no brother, yet he is
> always working, never satisfied with the wealth he has. For whom

---

3. *Ecclesiastes* (Louisville: John Knox, 2000), p. 50.

is he working so hard and denying himself any pleasure? This is useless *[hevel]*, too — and a miserable way to live. (TEV)

Notice the way that the book's thematic word, *hevel*, frames this section. The same sentiment, warning against a lifestyle that is obsessed with work, is expressed in Psalm 127:

> It is in vain that you rise up early and go late to rest,
>   eating the bread of anxious toil;
> for he gives sleep to his beloved.

(Ps 127:2)

The best commentary I have found on both of these texts is a piece written by columnist Ellen Goodman, describing Phil, a workaholic:

Boston. He worked himself to death, finally and precisely at 3 a.m. Sunday. The obituary didn't say that, of course. It said that he died of a coronary thrombosis — I think that was it — but every one of his friends and acquaintances knew it instantly. He was a perfect Type A, a workaholic, a classic, they said to each other and shook their heads — and thought for five or 10 minutes about the way they lived.

This man who worked himself to death finally and precisely at 3 a.m. Sunday — on his day off — was 51 years old and he was a vice president. He was, however, one of the six vice presidents, and one of three who might conceivably — if the president died or retired soon enough — have moved to the top spot. Phil knew that.

He worked six days a week, five of them until 8 or 9 at night, during a time when his own company had begun the four-day week for everyone but the executives. He worked like the important people. He had no outside "extracurricular interests," unless, of course, you think about a monthly golf game that way. To Phil, it was work. He always ate egg-salad sandwiches at his desk. He was, of course, overweight, by 20 or 25 pounds. He thought it was OK, though, because he didn't smoke.

On Saturdays Phil wore a sports jacket to the office instead of a suit, because it was the weekend. He had a lot of people working for him, maybe 60, and most of them liked him most of the time. Three of them will be seriously considered for his job. The obituary didn't mention that. But it did list his "survivors" quite accurately. He is survived by his wife, Helen, 48 years old, a good woman of no particular marketable skills, who worked in an office before marrying and mothering. She had, according to her daughters, given up trying to compete with his work years ago, when the children were small. A company friend said, "I know how much you will miss him." And she answered, "I already have."

"Missing him all these years," she must have given up part of herself which had cared too much for the man. She would be "well taken care of." His "dearly beloved" eldest of the "dearly beloved" children is a hard-working executive in a manufacturing firm down South. In the day and a half before the funeral, he went around the neighborhood researching his father, asking the neighbors what he was like. They were embarrassed.

His second child was a girl, who is 24 and newly married. She lives near her mother and they are close, but whenever she was alone with her father, in a car driving somewhere, they had nothing to say to each other.

The youngest is 20, a boy, a high school graduate who has spent the last couple of years, like a lot of his friends, doing enough odd jobs to stay in grass and food. He was the one who tried to grab at his father, and tried to mean enough to him to keep the man at home.

He was his father's favorite. Over the last two years, Phil stayed up nights worrying about the boy. The boy once said, "My father and I only board here."

At the funeral, the 60-year-old company president told the 48-year-old widow that the 51-year-old deceased had meant much to the company and would be missed and would be hard to replace. The widow didn't look him in the eye. She was afraid he would read her bitterness and, after all, she would need him to straighten out the finances — the stock options and all that.

Phil was overweight and nervous and worked too hard. If he wasn't at the office, he was worried about it. Phil was a Type A, a heart-attack natural. You could have picked him out in a minute from a lineup. So when he finally worked himself to death, at precisely 3 a.m. Sunday, no one was really surprised.

By 5 p.m. the afternoon of the funeral, the company president had begun, discreetly of course, with care and taste, to make inquiries about his replacement. One of three men. He asked around, "Who's been working the hardest?"[4]

Qohelet's question remains: "For whom is he working so hard and denying himself any pleasure?" And his observation is worth considering, too: "This is useless [*hevel*] too — and a miserable way to live" (4:8 TEV).

Life Together (Ecclesiastes 4:9-12)

[9]Two are better off than one, because together they can work more effectively. [10]If one of them falls down, the other can help him up. But if someone is alone and falls, it's just too bad, because there is no one to help him. [11]If it is cold, two can sleep together and stay warm, but how can you keep warm by yourself? [12]Two men can resist an attack that would defeat one man alone. A rope made of three cords is hard to break. (TEV)

Chapter 4 began with a doubled lament, "with no one to comfort them," over the situation of the poor and homeless. They are alone, with no one to watch over them and no one to care for them, should they be involved in an accident (4:1-3). Here Qoheleth picks up the other side of the same theme, now speaking of the positive benefits of a life lived in connection with others.

The advantages of life together with another person is the theme

4. *Minneapolis Tribune,* 12 October 1976, p. 7A.

expressed in this section. Swimmers know about the "buddy system" at camps, where participants are divided into pairs and assigned to keep track of one other person. When the lifeguard blows the whistle, all who are in the water find their partners and raise hands, held together. The Teacher is commending something like that here (vv. 9-10). When the aging King David lay shivering with cold in his bed at night, his staff members found the young woman Abishag, and the king learned the meaning of that 1940s pop song, "I've Got My Love to Keep Me Warm" (v. 11; see 1 Kgs 1:1-4). Finally, in a world in which muggings, robberies, and rapes must have been as much a problem as they are in our own time, life together with a partner is a life that is less subject to danger (v. 12).

Better a Poor but Wise Youth (Ecclesiastes 4:13-16)

> ¹⁴A man may rise from poverty to become king of his country, or go from prison to the throne, but if in his old age he is too foolish to take advice, he is not as well off as a young man who is poor but intelligent. ¹⁵I thought about all the people who live in this world, and I realized that somewhere among them there is a young man who will take the king's place. ¹⁶There may be no limit to the number of people a king rules; when he is gone, no one will be grateful for what he has done. It is useless *[hevel]*. It is like chasing the wind. (TEV)

The Teacher's down-to-earth advice continues. "With gray hair comes wisdom," runs the old saying, but Qoheleth says, "It ain't necessarily so." Age does not inevitably guarantee wisdom. Young Elihu waited until three senior citizens had spoken their pieces concerning Job's suffering (Job 32:4) and then observed, "It is not the old that are wise, nor the aged that understand what is right" (v. 9). Ecclesiastes 4:13 states the thesis, "Better is a poor but wise youth than an old but foolish king" (NRSV), which is then followed by two examples. The NRSV translates verse 14 more literally than the TEV quoted above:

"One can indeed come out of prison to reign," thus calling to mind Joseph's rise to power in Egypt (Genesis 37–50). The truth of the observation in verse 15 is apparent to all observers of the political scene. No one is irreplaceable. New and better leaders emerge!

In sum, in this chapter Qoheleth offers a collection of observations and advice on matters of everyday living. The powerless and the poor will always be with us, as Jesus observed (Matt 26:11 and parallels). The prophets, the wisdom teachers, and the psalms make clear that one of the obligations and opportunities for the people of God is to become caretakers and advocates for the powerless (Isaiah, Amos, and others; see my book, *The Prophets and the Powerless*). Life together with another has advantages over life without friends or family. When one's work becomes all-consuming, work can become demonic and destructive. Thomas Krüger points out that for Qoheleth, "Work and toil cannot produce happiness in the form of pleasure and enjoyment, but pleasure and enjoyment can be part of work and toil"[5] (see also 3:13, 22; 5:18; 9:9). Leaders, including political leaders, may become corrupt.

Oppression, envy, greed, overwork, foolishness — such are the everyday, earthly things with which Ecclesiastes 4 is concerned. And in the background that pedal note, *hevel,* is droning on. We hear it four times, drowning out any sounds of joy (vv. 4, 7, 8, 16).

---

5. *Qoheleth* (Minneapolis: Fortress, 2004), p. 4, on Eccl 8:15.

5 What about God?
Ecclesiastes 5

This statement is the interpreter of the entire book: Solomon intends to forbid vain anxieties, so that we may happily enjoy the things that are present and not care at all about the things that are in the future, lest we permit the present moment, our moment, to slip away.

Martin Luther, commenting on Ecclesiastes 5:18-20,
in *Notes on Ecclesiastes*, p. 93

It is said that in a country of sharp contrasts, no one can sleep. The poor — the majority — do not sleep because they are hungry, and the rich do not sleep because they know it.

Elsa Tamez on Ecclesiastes 5:12, *When the Horizons Close*, p. 82

The fourth chapter of Ecclesiastes offered considerations of earthly things, a variety of matters that were "under the sun" (4:1, 3, 7, 15). Now in this fifth chapter the Teacher gives some instruction about heavenly things, that is, about God. Ecclesiastes 5 consists of two outer sections, each of which speaks about God (vv. 1-7, referring to God six times, and vv. 18-20, with four references to God), and a middle section that is concerned about things on earth, making no mention of God (vv. 8-17). The chapter as a whole may be understood as an explication of the statement in verse 2: "God is in heaven [vv. 1-7, 18-20] and you upon earth" (vv. 8-17). The chapter concludes with a fourth, ringing affirmation of the book's "joy" theme [vv. 18-20; so far also 2:24-26; 3:12-13, 22].

God Is in Heaven (Ecclesiastes 5:1-7)

¹Guard your steps when you go to the house of God; to draw near to listen is better than the sacrifice offered by fools; for they do not know how to keep from doing evil. ²Never be rash with your mouth, nor let your heart be quick to utter a word before God, for God is in heaven, and you upon earth; therefore let your words be few.

³For dreams come with many cares, and a fool's voice with many words.

⁴When you make a vow to God, do not delay fulfilling it; for he has no pleasure in fools. Fulfill what you vow. ⁵It is better that you should not vow than that you should vow and not fulfill it. ⁶Do not let your mouth lead you into sin, and do not say before the messenger that it was a mistake; why should God be angry at your words, and destroy the work of your hands?

⁷With many dreams come vanities and a multitude of words; but fear God.

Now, for the first time in the book of Ecclesiastes, the reader is directly addressed. Notice the imperative verbs framing this section ("*Guard* your steps," v. 1; "*fear* God," v. 7) and the series of verbs with an imperative sense: "*Guard* your steps" (v. 1); "Never *be rash* with your mouth, nor *let* your heart *be quick*" (v. 2); "*do* not *delay* in fulfilling" (v. 4); "*do* not *let* your mouth *lead* you into sin" (v. 6); "but *fear* God" (v. 7). These verbs indicate that *instruction* is taking place. Here the Teacher is teaching. The topic for the lesson, which we could imagine the Teacher printing in capital letters on the blackboard, is announced in verse 2: GOD IS IN HEAVEN AND YOU UPON EARTH. We can imagine the Teacher listing these themes on the board:

Verse 1: Listening

The "when you go" of verse 1 assumes that the readers do go regularly to worship. It also assumes that there is something to hear ("to listen") on this occasion of worship in the temple. There would be songs and prayers and readings from Scripture and the interpreting of Scripture in the form of instruction or sermon. The "better than" saying (see the similar sayings in chs. 4 and 7) of verse 1 speaks of the merits of listening. "Faith comes from what is heard," Paul would one day write (Rom 10:17). Luther spoke of the church as *Mundhaus* ("mouthhouse"), that is, a place where speaking and listening take place.

Verse 1: Sacrifices

This section of the Teacher's instruction assumes that sacrifices are going on at the place of worship. The instruction given here does not call for putting an end to sacrifices, nor does it suggest boycotting worship services. Rather, the individual is advised to participate in these activities intelligently and with understanding, and to tolerate practices of others, even if they are foolish![1]

The biblical tradition has a history of warning against reducing religion to the offering of sacrifices in a mechanical sort of way, or against thinking that cultic activity could be substituted for obedience. When Saul took for himself the conquered enemy's cattle and sheep, disobeying the rules of holy war, claiming that he was going to offer them as a sacrifice to the Lord, the prophet Samuel confronted him (1 Sam 15:10-33):

---

1. Thomas Krüger, *Qoheleth* (Minneapolis: Fortress, 2004), p. 107.

Has the LORD as great delight in burnt offerings and sacrifices,
> as in obeying the voice of the LORD?
Surely, to obey is better than sacrifice,
> and to heed than the fat of rams.

(v. 22)

It seems that in ancient Israel there was also the danger of thinking one could substitute sacrifices for the doing of justice. But the writer of Proverbs puts the matter quite clearly: "To do righteousness and justice is more acceptable to the LORD than sacrifice" (Prov 21:3). It was the great prophets of the eighth century B.C.E., however, who most clearly made the point that religion cannot be reduced to ritual, at the expense of social justice. Amos speaks in the name of the Lord, who says:

I hate, I despise your festivals,
> and I take no delight in your solemn assemblies.
Even though you offer me your burnt offerings and grain
>> offerings,
> I will not accept them;
and the offerings of well-being of your fatted animals
> I will not look upon.
Take away from me the noise of your songs;
> I will not listen to the melody of your harps.
But let justice roll down like waters,
> and righteousness like an ever-flowing stream.
>> (Amos 5:21-24; see also Isa 1:10-17; Mic 6:6-8; Hos 6:6)

Like the Teacher whose words we find here in Ecclesiastes, the prophets do not advocate doing away with the practices of worship. But they do call for reforming them and coupling them with a concern for the widow, the orphan. and the poor.[2]

---

2. On this theme, see my book, *The Prophets and the Powerless.*

Verse 2: Words, Words, Words

According to the Bible, one of the marks of the person who is wise is that he or she is careful with words. When praying in public, says the Teacher, "let your words be few" (5:2). This statement sounds like similar advice given in Proverbs, about words in general. The wisdom writers warn against too much talking:

> One who spares words is knowledgeable;
>   one who is cool in spirit has understanding.
> Even fools who keep silent are considered wise;
>   when they close their lips, they are deemed intelligent.
>
> (17:27-28)

Proverbs also warns against substituting talking for action: "In all toil there is profit, but mere talk leads only to poverty" (14:23) and advises against uniformed blathering: "A fool takes no pleasure in understanding, but only in expressing personal opinion" (18:2). The wrong words can get one in trouble: "To watch over mouth and tongue is to keep out of trouble" (21:23). But speaking the right word at the right time can be a moment of beauty, "A word fitly spoken is like apples of gold in a setting of silver" (25:11). In his comments on the Joseph story, which exhibits a good number of themes typical to wisdom literature, Gerhard von Rad observes that Joseph's brothers provide a negative example in the use of words. When they are invited to dine at the home of a man whom they believe to be a high ranking Egyptian official (Genesis 43), "Once in the front door they begin to talk."[3]

Standing in this wisdom tradition of considered and conservative use of words, Ecclesiastes warns against mindless verbosity: "fools talk on and on" says 10:14. Here, the Teacher is concerned about the use of words when speaking to God, that is, when praying. "Be careful with what you say to God," the Teacher is saying. "Never be rash

---

3. Gerhard von Rad, *Genesis* (Philadelphia: Westminster, 1961), p. 383.

with your mouth, nor let your heart be quick to utter a word before God." "Think before you speak" is the TEV translation. Qoheleth's instruction is given a reason: "for God is in heaven, and you upon earth; therefore let your words be few." This puts things in the proper perspective. The prophet of the Exile once put it this way:

> For my thoughts are not your thoughts,
>   nor are your ways my ways, says the LORD.
> For as the heavens are higher than the earth,
>   so are my ways higher than your ways
>   and my thoughts than your thoughts.
>
> (Isa. 55:8-9)

Jesus also had things to say about the use of words in prayer. He warned against public prayers that are overly long-winded, pointing to the bad example of hypocrites who "love to stand and pray in the synagogues and at the street corners, so that they may be seen by others" (Matt 6:5). Jesus recommended concise public prayers: "When you are praying, do not heap up empty phrases as the Gentiles do; for they think that they will be heard because of their many words" (Matt 6:7). The most well-known public prayer that Jesus has given to followers is the Lord's Prayer, which is very short (Matt 6:9-13). But Jesus also taught that there is a time for private prayers (Matt 6:6), and these prayers may indeed be lengthy, as Jesus exemplified in his prayers in Gethsemane (Mark 14:32-42 and parallels).

"God is in heaven, and you upon earth; therefore let your words be few" (5:2). It can be that, in our own situations, we tend to reverse the practice of Jesus. There are overenthusiastic clerics and worship leaders who love to pray at great length in public, and there are also interminable litanies and liturgies that test the patience and piety of even the most faithful believers. On the other hand, the practice of disciplined private prayer is often a difficult one to maintain. Dietrich Bonhoeffer, the German pastor who was martyred because of his role in the plot against Hitler's life, wrote about the discipline of private daily Bible reading and prayer which he called the "secret discipline" (or "arcane discipline") in his books, *Life Together* and *Letters and Papers from Prison*. Bonhoeffer was calling for both the maintaining of the secret discipline and participating in political events of one's time. He once put it this way: "The secret discipline without worldly involvement ends up in a ghetto. But worldly involvement without the secret discipline is just so much sham and noise" (German . . . *ist nur noch Boulevard*).[4]

Verses 4-5: Words and Vows

A vow is a conditional promise to do something for God if God does something for the one making the vow, ordinarily using "if . . . then" language: "God, if you will do this, then I promise to do that." Thus Hannah promises that if the Lord gives her a son, she will dedicate that son to the Lord's service:

> She made this vow: "O LORD of hosts, if only you will look on the misery of your servant, and remember me, and not forget your servant, but will give to your servant a male child, then I will set him before you as a nazirite until the day of his death." (1 Sam 1:11)

Deuteronomy has a directive about taking such a vow seriously:

> If you make a vow to the LORD your God, do not postpone fulfilling it; for the LORD your God will surely require it of you, and you would incur guilt. But if you refrain from vowing, you will not incur guilt. (Deut 23:21-22)

And the Teacher advises here that if you make a vow, you should fulfill it (5:4-5).

In sum: This section tells us a good deal about the Teacher's view of God. Qoheleth is obviously no atheist, denying God's existence.

---

4. See Eberhard Bethge, *Dietrich Bonhoeffer: Eine Biographie* (Munich: Chr. Kaiser, 1967), p. 992.

He is, in fact, concerned about proper worship of God, here described in terms of listening, making offerings, prayer, and also keeping vows. The emphasis is on God's otherness and majesty (5:2), but also expressed is the conviction that this "wholly other" God acts in the affairs of humans (v. 6). According to the Teacher, God is concerned about the words of one's mouth (v. 2) and also the works of one's hands (v. 6). And then comes the Teacher's own words of counsel, after his discussion about "God in heaven": "Fear God." This expression does not mean to be afraid of God, but to have respect for God, much as a child has respect for a loving parent. The same instruction appears at the conclusion of the entire book: "Have reverence for God, and obey his commands" (12:13 TEV; see also 3:14 [NRSV "awe"]; 7:18 [TEV "have reverence for"]; 8:12, 13).

You Are on Earth (Ecclesiastes 5:8-17)

8If you see in a province the oppression of the poor and the violation of justice and right, do not be amazed at the matter; for the high official is watched by a higher, and there are yet higher ones over them. 9But all things considered, this is an advantage for a land: a king for a plowed field.

10The lover of money will not be satisfied with money; nor the lover of wealth, with gain. This also is vanity.

11When goods increase, those who eat them increase; and what gain has their owner but to see them with his eyes?

12Sweet is the sleep of laborers, whether they eat little or much; but the surfeit of the rich will not let them sleep.

13There is a grievous ill that I have seen under the sun: riches were kept by their owners to their hurt, 14and those riches were lost in a bad venture; though they are parents of children, they have nothing in their hands. 15As they came from their mother's womb, so they shall go again, naked as they came; they shall take nothing for their toil, which they may carry away with their hands. 16This also is a grievous ill: just as they came, so shall they go; and what gain do they have from toiling for the wind? 17Besides, all their days they eat in darkness, in much vexation and sickness and resentment.

After this instruction about God and heavenly things (5:1-7), the Teacher now comes down to some observations about humans and practical matters, addressing "you upon earth" (5:2).

Ecclesiastes 5:8-9 reflects Qoheleth's concern for the poor and the justice due them (see also 4:1-3 and the comments in connection with that passage). His hope is that the governmental system of checks and balances will correct the oppression of the poor.

Three sayings in 5:10-12 continue to be concerned about poverty and riches. (1) According to verse 10, the lover of money is never satisfied, says the Teacher. The old slogan on a box of Cracker Jack, a confection of our childhood, said, "The more you eat, the more you want." The same is true, according to the Teacher, when it comes to money (see also 1 Tim 6:10, which is often misquoted as "money is the root of all evil"). (2) The observation in verse 11 is about "freeloaders."[5] The TEV translates, "The richer you are, the more mouths you have to feed." (3) Finally, the Teacher observes that worry over properties and finances will often rob a rich person of a good night's sleep (v. 12). Qoheleth was concerned about such a basic human need as sleep, and connected insomnia and worry over business affairs (8:16). Another teacher, Jesus ben Sirach, says something similar about anxiety and sleep:

Wakefulness over wealth wastes away one's flesh,
and anxiety about it drives away sleep.
Wakeful anxiety prevents slumber,
and a severe illness carries off sleep.

Sirach goes on to give what sounds like quite modern advice:

5. See the note in the *HarperCollins Study Bible,* edited by Wayne A. Meeks (New York: HarperCollins, 1993), p. 992.

Healthy sleep depends on moderate eating;
    he rises early, and feels fit.
The distress of sleeplessness and of nausea
    and colic are with the glutton.

(Sir 31:1-2, 20)

My teacher and friend Gerhard Frost said to me one morning, "I just had one of those nights when I was lying awake, baby-sitting the world." Psalm 127 says, in effect, "Relax. Have a good sleep. You can let God take care of the world for one night!" The writer of Psalm 127 calls a good night's sleep a gift of God:

It is vain that you rise up early
    and go late to rest,
enjoying the bread of anxious toil;
    for he gives sleep to his beloved.

(Ps 127:2)

I have appreciated what Charles Péguy says about the subject in his poem entitled "Sleep." God is speaking and says:

Sleep is perhaps the most beautiful thing I have created.
And I myself rested on the seventh day.

Poor people, they don't know what is good.
They look after their business very well during the day.
But they haven't enough confidence in me
    to let me look after it during the night.
As if I wasn't capable of looking after it during one night.

And I say Blessed, blessed is the man
who puts off what he has to do until tomorrow.
Blessed is he who puts off. That is to say, Blessed is he who hopes.
    And who sleeps.

(*Basic Verities*)

Finally, see the comment of Elsa Tamez, a professor at the Biblical University in Costa Rica, on Eccl 5:12 at the head of this chapter.

The material in 5:13-17 continues the Teacher's instruction about wealth, now in the form of a story formulated as the result of a personal observation: "There is a grievous ill that I have seen under the sun" (that is, on earth). The Teacher has observed certain persons who have hoarded their riches and then lost them all in a bad investment or a stock market crash. In contrast to the example cited in 4:7-8, these persons do have heirs, but have nothing left to pass on to them. They ought to have known the truth of what Job said after he had lost his family and his property: "Naked I came from my mother's womb, and naked shall I return there" (Job 1:21). The Teacher here is using a story to make a point; he has seen the situation and draws a lesson from it.

For Qoheleth, "the most tangible setting for joy is found around a table."[6] This is also true for the Bible in general. There are a good many pictures of Jesus enjoying table fellowship with friends during his working days and also in the next life (Matt 8:11 and parallels; Rev 19:9). Another example: Jesus says, "Listen! I am standing at the door, knocking; if you hear my voice and open the door, I will come in to you and eat with you, and you with me" (Rev 3:20). But if table fellowship is an occasion for joy, it can also be a setting for sadness and sorrow. This segment ends with a distressing picture of persons gathered at a table, eating in the darkness, suffering from illness, and hating one another: "They are always gloomy at mealtime, and they are troubled, sick, and bitter" (5:17 CEV).

After this gloomy scene, the final segment of Ecclesiastes 5 concludes with another picture of table fellowship, this time marked by an atmosphere of joy.

6. William P. Brown, *Ecclesiastes* (Louisville: John Knox, 2000), p. 128.

"The Joy, Joy, Joy, Joy, Down in My Heart"
(Ecclesiastes 5:18-20)

> 18This is what I have seen to be good: it is fitting to eat and drink
> and find enjoyment in all the toil with which one toils under the
> sun the few days of the life God gives us; for this is our lot.
> 19Likewise all to whom God gives wealth and possessions and
> whom he enables to enjoy them, and to accept their lot and find en-
> joyment in their toil — this is the gift of God. 20For they will
> scarcely brood over the days of their lives, because God keeps them
> occupied with the joy of their hearts.

The theme of this chapter is "What about God?" The Hebrew word
Elohim, translated "God," occurs more often in Ecclesiastes 5 than
anywhere else in the book. The three-part structure of the chapter is
instructive. It begins with a picture of God who "is in heaven" (5:2), or
"our Father who is in heaven" as Jesus put it (Matt 6:9), and continues
with the Teacher's instruction about relating to that God in worship
and prayer and attitude (5:1-7). The chapter goes on to words addressed to "you upon earth" (v. 2), reminding hearers and readers
where we live our lives, and showing us some pictures of problems on
this earth, especially the gap between the rich and the poor (vv. 8-17).
Now the chapter concludes by indicating how God bridges the gap
between God in heaven and humans on earth (vv. 18-20).

The middle section ended with a gloomy picture of persons eating in the darkness, plagued by illness, filled with resentment (5:17).
But in verses 18-20 the mood changes. We hear again of table fellowship, but this time there's a party going on. Those participating are
enjoying the meal and also find enjoyment in their everyday work on
this earth (the sense of "under the sun"). The next words show how
God makes the connection between heaven and earth: the pleasures
of eating and drinking and of engaging in enjoyable work are all
things that *God gives us* (v. 18). Then the Teacher, emphasizing the lesson with repetition, goes over it one more time: *God gives* wealth and
possessions and work that is enjoyable. And finally, speaking of all

these things, the Teacher says a third time, "this is the *gift of God*" (v. 19). We have heard the same themes before, in the "enjoy" passages of 2:24-26; 3:12-13, 22. More of such passages will follow.

God's people are encouraged to enjoy their work and their wealth each day of their lives. When they reflect on the problems in the world around them (5:8-17) they won't have time to worry and brood, because "God keeps them occupied with the joy in their hearts." At this point in the classroom instruction which this chapter records, we could imagine the Teacher pausing and calling for a chorus of the Gospel song, "I've got the joy, joy, joy, joy down in my heart."

The JPS Version translates 5:20 as, "For such a man will not brood much over the days of his life, because God keeps him busy enjoying himself." Jesus also counseled against brooding overmuch about life on this earth and its cares. As Qoheleth does, Jesus points away from earthly cares to God's heavenly caring:

> Look at the birds of the air; they neither sow nor reap nor gather into barns, and yet your heavenly Father feeds them. Are you not of more value than they? (Matt 6:26)

The birds, apparently, do not brood over the days of their lives. They go on doing what birds are designed to do and do not allow worries about the future to rob them of their song.

Finally, we return to Luther's comment on Eccl 5:18-20, cited at the beginning of this chapter. Luther makes a bold, comprehensive interpretive statement here, declaring that these verses furnish the clue for understanding the book of Ecclesiastes as a whole. The book, says Luther, is a call to avoid anxiety, to embrace joy in the everyday present where we live, and to leave the future in God's hands.

In the words of 5:18-20, we hear summarized what the Teacher has to say in the entire book of Ecclesiastes. With that sustained pedal point still sounding in the background (v. 10, "This also is vanity [*hevel*]"), the Teacher counsels living fully each day of one's life, one day at a time, enjoying God's gifts and enjoying one's work. We shall hear more on this "enjoy" theme in Chapter 7 below.

What Does Ecclesiastes Say about God?

At this point we may pause to ask: What is this Teacher's under-standing of God? Since Ecclesiastes 5 is the place in the book where the most concentrated statements about God are found, with a total of 10 occurrences of the word, it seems a good place to summarize what these statements indicate about the Teacher's theology, or un-derstanding of God. We shall put together a sketch of Qoheleth's theology from Ecclesiastes 5 and then fill in this sketch with further references to God from the entire book. When the Teacher speaks of God, he also speaks about humans and how life ought to be lived; thus we consider these topics as well.

The word that the book of Ecclesiastes uses for God is not Yahweh, the personal name given to Moses (Exod 3:13-15) and used throughout the Old Testament. Rather, the Hebrew term *Elohim* is used, which is a general designation for the Deity (like the English God or god) or also a personal name (God). To summarize what Qoheleth says about God, humans, and human living, note the fol-lowing points:

1. "God is in heaven" (5:2). God is distant but concerned
about matters on earth.
The sense of this statement is that God is "wholly other," far distant from humans. Isaiah spoke of the Lord who is "high and lofty" (Isa 6:1) and "holy," which means separate or distant (6:3). The prophet of the Exile spoke of the mystery attending the ways of the Lord (Isa 55:6-9). Jesus taught his followers to pray, "Our Father *in heaven*" (Matt 6:9). God, says Eccl 3:11, has made everything beautiful. What God does endures, and all should be in awe of God (3:14) and worship God in humility and reverence (5:1-2, 7).

While distant, this God has concern for things happening on earth. God is the Maker of everything on earth (3:11; 7:13). God gives human beings their lives (5:18; 8:15), is their Maker and Creator (7:29; 12:1), and takes life back (12:7). God assigns people certain activities (1:13; 3:10) and may give them wealth, possessions, and honor (5:19;

6:2). God controls the events of history, giving both days of prosperity and days of adversity (7:14), even allowing bad things to happen to people (6:2). God tests humans (3:18) and will judge them (3:17; 11:9; 12:14). God has done much, but God's works are not understandable for humans (8:17).

Psalm 113 provides a good expression of these two dimensions in the biblical understanding of God:

1 Praise the LORD!
   Praise, O servants of the LORD;
      praise the name of the LORD.
2 Blessed be the name of the LORD
      from this time on and forevermore.
3 From the rising of the sun to its setting
      the name of the LORD is to be praised.
4 The LORD is high above all nations,
      and his glory above the heavens.
5 Who is like the LORD our God,
      who is seated on high,
6 who looks far down
      on the heavens and the earth?
7 He raises the poor from the dust,
      and lifts the needy from the ash heap,
8 to make them sit with princes,
      with the princes of his people.
9 He gives the barren woman a home,
      making her the joyous mother of children.
   Praise the LORD!

First, the psalm makes clear God's *might*. The psalm calls for God to be praised throughout all time (Ps 113:2) and through all space (v. 3). This God is "high above all nations" and without peer (vv. 4-5). The psalm continues by also making clear that God cares about individual persons on this earth, that is, by speaking of God's *mercy*. It portrays God as looking down at the problems of the poor, then restoring the poor person to a place of honor in the community (vv. 6-8). The psalm concludes with a picture of a young woman, who had not been able to have children but who now has been given children and is playing happily with them in her home (v. 9). The table prayer says, "God is great, God is good, and we thank God for this food." Those two dimenions of greatness and goodness, might and mercy are clearly articulated in this psalm and also in Ecclesiastes.

2. "And you upon earth" (5:2). Humans are creatures of the earth, plagued with problems and conflict.

The Teacher recognizes that there are problems with this earthly existence in which we humans participate. There is the difficulty of finding meaning in life. When work, wisdom, or pleasure is raised to the rank of one's reason for living — that is, made one's ultimate concern or one's god — all are ultimately unsatisfying. Each of these ends up as disappointing, as futility or *hevel* (Ecclesiastes 1–2). There are more problems. Consider the injustices in human life (3:16-17): poor people are oppressed (4:1-3; 5:8-9); people are greedy and lovers of money (5:10-17); a person may gather many possessions and wealth and honor, but then die and leave all for a stranger to enjoy (6:1-6); life isn't fair and people don't get what they deserve (7:15-18; 8:14; 9:11-12); ordinary people don't get the leaders they deserve (10:5-7, 16); death finally comes to all (2:14-17; 3:19-21; 6:3-6; 7:2; 12:1-8). And finally, studying, thinking, and writing about all these things is brain-breaking work (12:12)!

3. "So you do not know the work of God" (11:5). There is a bad connection between earth and heaven.

God is in heaven and people are on earth, but according to Qoheleth, all is not right with the world. To use an image from the world of communication: it is as if the picture on the TV screen has gone to black and the announcer says, "We have lost our signal." But the bad connection about which the Teacher speaks is the connection between humans and God! We humans don't know what God is doing, and we can't seem to find out. We can't seem to get through to God!

Our prayers don't seem to get off the ground! This theme comes up often in Ecclesiastes. Humans cannot find out what God has done or will do (3:10-11). Even though they work hard at trying to understand (12:12), they can't figure out what on earth God is doing. They can't predict the future (7:14). Though certain experts, presumably theologians and philosophers, claim to know all about God, they don't understand the ways of God either (8:16-17)! None of us really knows what God is up to (11:5). Such knowledge is too deep (7:24). Therefore, we humans shall have to learn to live with mystery, with unanswered questions (3:11b), and must remain in awe of God (3:14b; 5:2). As the Jewish Holocaust survivor Elie Wiesel has written and said on a number of occasions, "The questions remained questions, but somehow I could go on." It may be that we shall have to learn to live with mystery, with questions, even questions directed at God. After all, the "Why?" question that Jesus asked from the cross never received an answer (Mark 15:34)!

4. How then should we live? "Fear God. . . . It is fitting to eat and drink and find enjoyment in all the toil with which one toils under the sun. . . . This is the gift of God. . . . Fear God, and keep his commandments"
(5:7, 18-20; 12:13).

We have noted that in Ecclesiastes 5 Qoheleth addresses hearers/readers directly for the first time. The imperative verbs here provide a clue to the sort of life style that the Teacher is commending. The first imperatives, in 5:1-7, have to do with *human relationships to God.* The instruction here commends approaching the place of worship with an attitude of quiet reverence rather than trampling noisily about, offering sacrifices and lengthy prayers. Amos, speaking in the Lord's name, put it clearly: "Take away from me the noise of your songs; I will not listen to the melody of your harps" (Amos 5:23).

The right attitude for earthlings to have toward God in heaven is summarized in the imperative that closes this section: "Fear God!" The sense of this expression is made clear through the variety of translations: "have reverence for God" (TEV); "respect and obey God" (CEV); "stand in awe of God" (NIV). The recommendation to "fear God" appears in 5:7 and again in the very last instruction in the book: "fear God, and keep his commandments" (12:13). This attitude denoting respect and reverence runs through the book, expressed with various forms of the Hebrew root *yare'* (3:14 [NRSV "awe"]; 5:7; 7:18; 8:12, 13; 12:13).

After speaking of "heavenly things" and one's relationship to God in the first part of Ecclesiastes 5, the Teacher concludes by speaking of "earthly things," that is, *human relationships to others*. The first of these earthly things that the Teacher raises is the matter of the poor, the powerless in society (5:8-12; see also above, pp. 55-59, 73-74). To think that wealth will bring happiness is to live in a way that is only headed toward disappointment, asking "Is that all there is?" (see Chapter 2 above). The Teacher then concludes his discussion of earthly things by commending times of celebration in table fellowship with others and enjoyment in one's work (5:18-20). In such times of enjoyment, humans come in contact with God, identified in this short section as the Giver of life (v. 18), of wealth and possessions, of work that is enjoyable, and of joy down in their hearts (vv. 19-20).

Moving beyond Ecclesiastes 5, we hear more of Qoheleth's advice for daily living: *Enjoy the good days* (7:14)! Enjoy the ordinary, earthly good things, because these are gifts of God, "from the hand of God" (2:24-26; 3:12-13, 22). Eat, drink, and enjoy the days that God gives you (8:15)! Enjoy good wine, the woman or man whom you love, and throw yourself into your work, because God approves of all these things (9:7-10). Enjoy the days of your youth (11:9-10) before you say "I have no pleasure" (12:1). The Teacher counsels finding enjoyment in the company of others at times of eating and drinking, in life together with others, and also in one's work. In these good experiences, the "bad connections" may be restored and one may sense that one is in contact with God, the Giver of good, earthly gifts.

6   What about Death?
Ecclesiastes 6 and 7

*Lasset die Kindlein zu mir kommen und wehret ihnen nicht; denn solchen ist
das Reich Gottes (Let the little children come to me; do not stop them; for it is
to such that the kingdom of God belongs).*

> Inscription on a tombstone, rural Hartford,
> South Dakota, the other side of which reports the
> death of seven children from diphtheria in 1894

Leichen Text Pred. 7.2 (Funeral text Eccl 7:2).

> Inscription on a grandfather's tombstone,
> Emden cemetery, rural Minnesota, 1916

*Some day a company of men will process out to a churchyard and lower a coffin and everyone will go home; but one will not come back, and that will be
me.*

> Karl Barth, *Dogmatics in Outline*, pp. 117-18

A Death Too Soon (Ecclesiastes 6:1-6)

> ¹There is an evil that I have seen under the sun, and it lies heavy upon humankind: ²those to whom God gives wealth, possessions, and honor, so that they lack nothing of all that they desire, yet God does not enable them to enjoy these things, but a stranger enjoys them. This is vanity; it is a grievous ill. ³A man may beget a hundred children, and live many years; but however many are the days of his years, if he does not enjoy life's good things, or has no burial, I say that a stillborn child is better off than he. ⁴For it comes into vanity and goes into darkness, and in darkness its name is covered; ⁵moreover it has not seen the sun or known anything; yet it finds rest rather than he. ⁶Even though he should live a thousand years twice over, yet enjoy no good — do not all go to one place?

Chapter 6 of Ecclesiastes begins with another portrait of a very wealthy person. Qoheleth has already told of a person who had been working hard and had accumulated great riches but then suddenly came to the realization that he was not going to be able to take it all with him when he died (2:18)! A couple of chapters later the Teacher tells again of a person who had great riches and an insatiable desire to add to them, but who then came to the realization that he had no one to whom he could leave all this wealth (4:8)! Here in Chapter 6 the Teacher again tells of a person who had accumulated great wealth and earned great honor, but who apparently has died too young to enjoy these things, and a "stranger" enjoys all this person has worked for. Qoheleth concludes by sounding the thematic note of the book: "it is useless *(hevel)*" (6:2 TEV; note *hevel* in vv. 4, 9). The tragic situation of an untimely death as described here is familiar to us all: the young president who is just getting things going at the institution he has been guiding and is suddenly taken away by a thrombosis; the brilliant scholar who is just coming into the harvest time for his own lifetime of research and is felled by a mysterious disease; the woman whose good humor and wise judgment have sparked many a program in the community and church, suddenly taken by cancer; the reader can add his or her examples. The loss of any such persons is indeed "a grievous ill" (6:2). Notice two details here: the person who had left this life too soon had all the good things that life had to offer, but never had a chance to enjoy them. In the light of this situation, the "enjoy life while you can" theme of Ecclesiastes 9 takes on special significance. Another detail: notice the importance placed on a proper burial (v. 3); this "burial" theme will be picked up in Ecclesiastes 7.

The Second Half (Ecclesiastes 6:10-12)

[10]Whatever has come to be has already been named, and it is known what human beings are, and that they are not able to dispute with those who are stronger. [11]The more words, the more vanity, so how is one the better? [12]For who knows what is good for mortals while they live the few days of their vain life, which they pass like a shadow? For who can tell them what will be after them under the sun?

What is of particular interest in Ecclesiastes 6 is a feature that helps to understand the structure of the entire book. The Hebrew text has a note in the margin after verse 9: "half the book in verses." Such notes occur along the way in the Hebrew Bible to help the copyists check the accuracy of their work. In this case, the note says that there are 220 verses before verse 10 and 220 verses after it. Illustrating the same matter, the Hebrew Bible leaves extra space between the last line of verse 9 and the first line of verse 10.

The point is that 6:10-12 can be considered as the introduction to the second half of the book of Ecclesiastes. One may observe that this half, from 6:10–12:14, is made up of shorter units than the first half. Verse 11 offers a typical Qoheleth comment about being careful with words, "The more words, the more *hevel*" (see 5:2, "therefore let your words be few"). Verse 12 raises two important questions: First, "Who knows what is good (Hebrew *tov*) for humans?" (for "Who knows?"

see Chapter 3 above). Qoheleth does not provide a simple answer. But in the segment that follows, 7:1-14, he lists a number of things that are "better than" others. The Hebrew is literally "more good," thus picking up the "good" theme introduced in 6:12. The second question raised in verse 12 is, "Who can tell what the future will bring?" The Teacher's answer to this question appears to be: Only God knows! The topic of the unknowability of the future comes up elsewhere also (see above on 3:11; 7:14, etc.).

Reflections on Some Tombstones (Ecclesiastes 7)

In the days when I did a good deal of substitute preaching, mostly in country churches in South Dakota, Minnesota, and Iowa, I always tried to arrive at the church an hour early to get settled into the place and prepared for the service. Whenever possible, a part of my preparation was to walk through the cemetery, ordinarily adjacent to the church. By reading the names and inscriptions on the tombstones, I could learn something of the history of the congregation and get a sense of who these people were.

This was always an interesting and informative exercise. For example, a couple of summers ago I was waiting for a service to begin and took a walk through a cemetery in rural Backus, in northern Minnesota. As I stopped to read the inscriptions on the grave markers, I noticed that a girl about 10 years old was observing me. Then she ran over to one of the tombstones and waved me over to her. When I got there she said, "This is my favorite one!" I could see why. Etched into the shiny black tombstone was neither a cross nor any sort of religious symbol, but rather a large replica of a semi-truck and trailer, complete with smokestack. The semi was cruising through the clouds. On the side of the trailer are the words "Driving for the Lord." "Cool!" said the 10-year-old, and I agreed. After I had preached, I shook hands with the trucker's widow at the door, and she told me about her deceased husband.

The stories told on these grave markers can be incredibly sad. I recall one on a tombstone adjacent to a country church outside of Hartford, South Dakota. Since this congregation had been founded by German pioneers, the older inscriptions were all in that language. On one marker was the tragic story of the death of a woman and seven small children, all within a period of a few weeks, in July 1894. When I checked with the pastor, he told me there had been a terrible diphtheria epidemic in that year. On the other side of the tombstone were words from the Gospel of Mark 10:14: "Let the little children come unto me; do not stop them; for it is to such as these that the kingdom of God belongs." I have returned to that country cemetery a number of times, and have always walked over to look at that tombstone. I could barely imagine the terrible tragedy. I thought of the grief of that South Dakota farm couple who had lost their seven children. And I imagined them going to the monument works, taking out a Bible, and telling the stone cutter to put that text on that grave marker. That tombstone continues to proclaim their faith!

Now a more personal reflection on a tombstone. It was a number of years ago that members of our family and some friends gathered at Emden cemetery, in rural Minnesota. Once a church had stood next to the cemetery, but with the advent of the automobile, the building was torn down and a new structure was built in the nearby town of Renville. We were there for the burial of my aunt. As we walked among the tombstones, we stopped by the graves where my mother's parents are buried. It was a cold, rainy April day. My mother told us the story of her father's death in 1916. He was a farmer and had been in the barn, feeding the horses. My mother, then eight years old, was sent out to get him for supper. She stepped into the barn and found him lying on the floor, feed spilled all around him. He was dead. Then she told of the funeral and the burial at this cemetery. "It was a rainy day like this. The horses were pulling the casket on a cart, and I still remember, it almost slipped off!" We stood there and I noticed, for the first time, the inscription on the tombstone. At the bottom was my grandfather's family name. Above, in large capital letters were the words:

LEICHEN TEXT
PRED. 7,2

Translated, that means: "Funeral text Ecclesiastes 7:2." (See p. xi above for a photograph.) I didn't recognize the text, and when we got home I looked it up. It says, in the KJV: "It is better to go to the house of mourning, than to go to the house of feasting: for that is the end of all men; and the living will lay it to his heart." I could imagine the sadness of two little girls, ages eight and ten, standing in the rain at their father's graveside. I wondered just why that preacher had chosen this text from Ecclesiastes, and what he had said. I thought for a moment of my own mortality, and Karl Barth's observation cited above: "but one will not come back, and that will be me." I made a resolve to begin an investigation of the book of Ecclesiastes in order to understand that inscription on my grandfather's tombstone. Then I began preaching, teaching and lecturing on Ecclesiastes in a variety of contexts (see pp. xii-xiii above).

Better to Attend a Funeral than a Party (Ecclesiastes 7:1-14)

1 A good name is better than precious ointment,
    and the day of death, than the day of birth.
2 It is better to go to the house of mourning
    than to go to the house of feasting;
  for this is the end of everyone,
    and the living will lay it to heart.
3 Sorrow is better than laughter,
    for by sadness of countenance the heart is made glad.
4 The heart of the wise is in the house of mourning;
    but the heart of fools is in the house of mirth.
5 It is better to hear the rebuke of the wise
    than to hear the song of fools.
6 For like the crackling of thorns under a pot,
    so is the laughter of fools;
    this also is vanity.

7   Surely oppression makes the wise foolish,
        and a bribe corrupts the heart.
8   Better is the end of a thing than its beginning;
        the patient in spirit are better than the proud in spirit.
9   Do not be quick to anger,
        for anger lodges in the bosom of fools.
10   Do not say, "Why were the former days better than these?"
        For it is not from wisdom that you ask this.
11   Wisdom is as good as an inheritance,
        an advantage to those who see the sun.
12   For the protection of wisdom is like the protection of money,
        and the advantage of knowledge is that wisdom gives
        life to the one who possesses it.
13   Consider the work of God;
        who can make straight what he has made crooked?
    14In the day of prosperity be joyful, and in the day of adversity
consider; God has made the one as well as the other, so that mortals may not find out anything that will come after them.

The first unit in Ecclesiastes 7 is verses 1-14, which includes a succes-
sion of *better than* sayings (vv. 1a, 1b, 2, 3, 5, 8a, 8b, 10a). This *better than*
formula is found throughout the Bible (see the examples on pp. 54-
55 above) and is especially characteristic of biblical Wisdom literature. Note also the following:

> *Better* is a dry morsel with quiet
>   *than* a house full of feasting with strife.
>
> (Prov 17:1)

> It is *better* to live in a corner of the housetop
>   *than* in a house shared with a contentious wife.
>
> (Prov 25:24)

Especially interesting is a collection of these *better than* sayings in Sir
40:18-30. For example:

Wine and music gladden the heart,
> but the love of friends is *better than* either.

> (v. 20)

A friend or companion is always welcome,
> but a sensible wife is *better than* either.

> (v. 23)

Gold and silver make one stand firm,
> but good counsel is esteemed *more than* either.

> (v. 25)

Riches and strength build up confidence,
> but the fear of the Lord is *better than* either.

> (v. 26)

Further examples of *better than* sayings occur in Ps 37:16; Prov 12:9; 16:8; 19:1; 27:5, 10b. Qoheleth asks the question, "Who knows what is good (Hebrew *tov*) for mortals?" (6:12). Ecclesiastes 7:1-14 does not give a simple answer to that question, but instead provides eight examples of things that are "more *tov*," that is, "more good" or "better than," others.

Why did the wisdom teachers use such a formula? First, they were teachers, and teachers are always looking for pedagogical devices to make the material they are teaching interesting and memorable. One can observe, for example, such devices as *parallelism,* where a statement is made and then a second statement is added to balance it, saying something similar *(synonymous parallelism):*

Through sloth the roof sinks in,
> and through indolence the house leaks.

> (10:18; also vv. 8, 9)

Or the second statement may say the opposite of the first *(antithetic parallelism):*

> Words spoken by the wise bring them favor,
>> but the lips of fools consume them.
>>> (10:12; also v. 2)

Or the second balancing statement may provide a *reason* for what is said in the first line:

> The toil of fools wears them out,
>> for they do not even know the way to town.
>>> (10:15; also 11:1)

Or the wisdom teachers may use *numerical devices,* such as the graduated numerical saying listing x things and then x + 1:

> Three things are too wonderful for me;
>> four I do not understand:
> the way of an eagle in the sky,
>> the way of a serpent on a rock,
> the way of a ship on the high seas,
>> and the way of a man with a girl.
>>> (Prov. 30:18-19; also vv. 21-23, 24-28, 29-31; 6:16-19)

In Eccl 11:2:

> Divide your means seven ways, or even eight,
>> for you do not know what disaster may happen on earth.

As for the *better than* sayings here in Ecclesiastes 7, this was another device to aid in memorization and no doubt in enjoyment. We can imagine a teacher quizzing students by asking, "What is better than the most expensive perfume that money can buy?" (7:1). The wisdom teachers must have found a certain intellectual and esthetic enjoyment in composing and arranging these sayings, the longest sequence of *better than* sayings in the Bible.

In what follows, we note especially the sayings that speak to the theme of this chapter, that is, what Qoheleth says about death. Ecclesiastes 7:1a says, "A good name is better than precious ointment." Other sayings from the Bible's Wisdom literature make the same point:

A good name is to be chosen rather than great riches.

(Prov 22:1)

The human body is a fleeting thing,
 but a virtuous name will never be blotted out.

Have regard for your name, since it will outlive you
 longer than a thousand hoards of gold.

The days of a good life are numbered,
 but a good name lasts forever.

(Sir 41:11-14; see also Job 18:17; Prov 10:7)

If the first half of 7:1 expresses a thought that occurs elsewhere in the biblical literature, the second half of the verse expresses a theme that is puzzling. What could the Teacher mean by this assertion that the day of death is better than the day of birth, a notion which is certainly counter to the usual "to life" spirit of the biblical writings, including the frequent directives to "enjoy" found in Ecclesiastes (see Chapter 7 below)?

There are a few hints elsewhere in this section as to what the Teacher is thinking. Verse 2 suggests that it is better to attend a funeral than a party. But why could this be? The last part of the verse suggests a reason: the CEV translates succinctly, "funerals remind us that we all must die." At a funeral, we can be reminded that we have all been given the gift of life "for a limited time only." That is, we are reminded that we are all mortal.

I recall a friend writing and telling about his first teaching job, at a small Midwestern college. "Our main problem," he wrote, "is our college president. He keeps getting himself confused with God." By that he meant that the president had forgotten that he, too, was a mortal whose wisdom and powers were limited, and whose life was of limited duration. Recall also the story that Jesus told about the wealthy farmer who kept buying more fields and amassing his fortune, forgetting that he was mortal. He said, "I'm going to buy up more fields and build more barns!" But during the night he learned that the next day he would die (Luke 12:13-21).

Funerals remind us that we ought not get ourselves confused with God. We ought to remember that, unlike God, we are not immortal. They are a reminder that one day each of us must die. We may recall the Latin motto, *memento mori,* "remember that we must die." Looking at life in this way tends to make us treasure and enjoy each day that we have. "This is the day that the LORD has made; let us rejoice and be glad in it," said the psalmist (Ps 118:24). To "lay to heart" (Eccl 7:2) means to put it in one's memory bank; note the same expression in 9:1.

"Sorrow is better than laughter," according to 7:3. The possible value of sorrow and suffering is a theme found elsewhere in Wisdom literature. Sadness and sorrow may be a part of the Lord's work of *disciplining:* "How happy is the one whom God reproves; therefore do not despise the discipline of the Almighty" (Job 5:17). See also Prov 3:11-12: "My child, do not despise the LORD's discipline or be weary of his reproof, for the LORD reproves the one he loves, as a father the son in whom he delights." Also Heb 12:6: "for the Lord disciplines those whom he loves." Or sorrow and suffering may be God's way of *testing* humans. See Wisd 3:5-6: "Having been disciplined a little, they will receive great good, because God tested them and found them worthy of himself; like gold in the furnace he tried them."

Verse 4 repeats the theme of verse 2. In the house of mourning, one might gain some insight about the brevity and therefore the preciousness of human life.

The sense of most of the sayings that follow in Ecclesiastes 7 is clear. Note the warning about idealizing the "good old days," a temptation that any of us can give in to (v. 10). Robert Gordis has a helpful comment on verses 13-14, which conclude this section:

This verse [7:13] and the following are an admirable epitome of Kohelet's thought — God is all-powerful, man must resign himself to ignorance regarding the meaning and purpose of life. Hence, he must take good and evil in his stride, enjoying the good while he can and remembering it during days of trouble.[1]

What Does Ecclesiastes Say about Death?

Since the theme of death is an important one in Ecclesiastes, it may be useful to gather together what the book as a whole has to say on the subject.

1. Qoheleth declares that death comes to all creatures,
humans and animals alike.
"For the fate of humans and the fate of animals is the same; as one dies, so dies the other. They all have the same breath *(ruach),* and humans have no advantage over the animals" (Eccl 3:19; compare Ps 49:12, 20). And further: "the same fate comes to all, to the righteous and the wicked, to the good and the evil, to the clean and the unclean, to those who sacrifice and those who do not sacrifice" (9:2-3).

2. Qoheleth assumes the importance of certain rituals
attending death and burial.
Ecclesiastes 7:2 speaks of a funeral service, apparently taking place in a home. The wise person, says the Teacher, will be present at that time of mourning (7:4) because he or she might learn something about his or her own mortality. Not to have a decent burial, says Qoheleth, would be a great loss: "A man may beget a hundred children, and live many years; but however many are the days of his years, if he does not enjoy life's good things, or has no burial, I say that a stillborn child is better off than he" (6:3). Note also Tob 4:3, where Tobit is speaking to his son Tobias about burial: "My son,

1. Robert Gordis, *Koheleth* (New York: Schocken, 1968), pp. 274-75.

when I die, give me a proper burial. Honor your mother and do not abandon her all the days of her life."

Sirach 38:16-23 advises mourning and grieving, but then being comforted and getting on with life!

> My child, let your tears fall for the dead,
>   and as one in great pain begin the lament.
> Lay out the body with due ceremony,
>   and do not neglect the burial.
>
> Let your weeping be bitter and your wailing fervent;
>   make your mourning worthy of the departed,
> for one day, or two, to avoid criticism;
>   then be comforted for your grief.
>
> For grief may result in death,
>   and a sorrowful heart saps one's strength. . . .
> When the dead is at rest, let his remembrance rest too,
>   and be comforted for him when his spirit has departed.

3. Qoheleth does not pretend to know everything about the ultimate fate of either humans or animals.

He expresses his own agnosticism on the matter with a characteristic "Who knows?": "Who knows whether the human spirit goes upward and the spirit of animals goes downward to the earth?" (3:21).

The Apostle Paul once wrote that there is much mystery in the question of what happens after human death (1 Cor 15:51). It was Reinhold Niebuhr who once suggested that God has not chosen to reveal to us humans "either the furniture of heaven or the temperature of hell."

4. Qoheleth points to the return of the breath/spirit
(see NRSV) to the Creator.

"Remember your creator in the days of your youth . . . before . . . the dust returns to the earth as it was, and the breath returns to God who gave it" (12:1, 7).

In sum: Qoheleth recognizes the universality of death and the value of traditional end-of-life practices. While he hints at a life beyond death with God, he does not claim to know any details about that life. But the last and final words from the Bible on these subjects have not been spoken by Ecclesiastes. We shall consider briefly some other biblical texts about death, and about resurrection:

What Does the Bible Say about Resurrection?

Qoheleth's observations about death, of course, should be considered in the context of what the Bible as a whole has to say about hope for life after death. In both Judaism and Christianity, that hope is expressed in terms of the resurrection of the body. The Greek word translated "body" in the New Testament is *sōma,* which refers to the whole person and could be well translated as "person." "I believe in the resurrection of the body, the life everlasting" is the way the Apostles' Creed puts it. The essential features of the biblical view of resurrection may be sketched as follows:

1. In the Old Testament, there are hints of a hope for life beyond death, in terms of hope for resurrection.
A few psalms articulate a hope for life beyond death. We have noted that the refrain of Psalm 49 declares that both humans and animals die (vv. 12, 20). But there is also a glimmer of hope for continuing life with God in this psalm, "But God will ransom my soul from the power of Sheol, for he will receive me" (v. 15). After wrestling with the question of why the evil prosper, the writer of Psalm 73 makes a first-person confession of faith:

> I was stupid and ignorant;
> I was like a brute beast toward you.
>
> Nevertheless I am continually with you;
> you hold my right hand.

> You guide me with your counsel,
>> and afterward you will receive me to glory.
>
>> (Ps 73:22-24 NRSV margin)

One commentator has named this psalm "The Great Nevertheless," rightly putting the focus on the importance of that word. Psalm 118:17, which Luther had printed on the wall of his study in the Wartburg Castle, put the matter this way: "I shall not die, but I shall live, and recount the deeds of the LORD."

Three chronologically later Old Testament texts express future hope in terms of resurrection. From the Isaiah Apocalypse (Isaiah 24–27), usually dated after the sixth-century Exile in Babylon, are two expressions of hope for resurrection:

> And [the LORD] will destroy on this mountain
>> the shroud that is cast over all peoples,
>> the sheet that is spread over all nations;
>> he will swallow up death forever.
> Then the Lord GOD will wipe away the tears from all faces,
>> and the disgrace of his people he will take away from
>>> all the earth,
>> for the LORD has spoken.
>
>> (Isa. 25:7-8)

There is another expression of resurrection hope in Isa 26:19, also a part of the postexilic Isaiah Apocalypse:

> Your dead shall live, their corpses shall rise.
>> O dwellers in the dust, awake and sing for joy!
>
>> (Isa. 26:19)

Finally, a text from Daniel, written in the second century B.C.E., expresses a clear hope for resurrection of the dead:

> Many of those who sleep in the dust of the earth shall awake, some to everlasting life, and some to shame and everlasting contempt.

Those who are wise shall shine like the brightness of the sky, and those who lead many to righteousness, like the stars forever and ever. (Dan 12:2-3)

2. The New Testament, written down in the light of the resurrection of Jesus, gives expression to a clear and confident hope in resurrection.

1 Corinthians 15 is the most focused and extensive expression of the Christian view of death and resurrection. Paul is arguing against certain persons in the Corinthian community who deny resurrection, saying "there is no resurrection of the dead" (v. 12). 1 Cor 15:3-7 is a tightly packed piece of early Christian preaching *(kerygma)*. Paul begins by indicating that what he is now passing on to these people in Corinth is teaching that he had previously received from members of the earliest church (15:3). These earliest witnesses declared that (1) Christ died for our sins; (2) this death was in accordance with Scripture; (3) Christ was buried and then raised on the third day, again "in accordance with the scriptures." Paul asserts that the announcement of Christ's resurrection from the dead was central to the Christian preaching from the beginning (15:11). He names some witnesses to whom the resurrected Christ had appeared: Cephas, the twelve apostles, 500 or so members of the earliest congregation, then James, the apostles, and Paul himself (1 Cor 15:1-11).

Continuing in his argumentative style, Paul grants these resurrection-deniers their point and then follows out the consequences. If indeed there is no resurrection of the dead, then Christ has not been raised and Christian preaching has been based on a lie (vv. 12-19). Then Paul shifts to the positive, asserting that Christ *has* been raised from the dead, as the "first fruits" of all the dead who will be raised (vv. 20-34).

Paul anticipates that someone in this young Corinthian congregation is going to ask about the nature of the resurrection body. His first reaction is to say, "that's a foolish question!" (v. 36). He continues with some illustrations to make his point: the present body (Greek *sōma*) is to the expected resurrection body as a seed is to a plant. The present body as buried is perishable, the resurrection body imperishable. To put it another way, the present body is buried in dishonor, but it will be raised in glory. Or yet another: it is buried in weakness, and will be raised in power.

How can this all be? Says the apostle, "I will tell you a mystery! We will not all die, but we will all be changed, in a moment, in the twinkling of an eye, at the last trumpet" (vv. 51-52).

The apostle does not know all the details of the transformation from the present body to the resurrection body. Like Qoheleth, at some points he has to say, "Who knows?" (Eccl 3:21)! For Paul, too, there remains some mystery (1 Cor 15:51-57).

3. An important clue for understanding the nature of the believer's resurrection body is the resurrection person of Jesus Christ.

The postresurrection texts tell us that while Christ's resurrection body was *not identical* with his preresurrection body, there was, however, *identity*. We could also speak in terms of *discontinuity* and *continuity*. When Jesus first appeared to Mary Magdalene in the Garden, she did not recognize him *(not identical; discontinuity)*, but when he said "Mary," she did and addressed him as Rabbouni ("Teacher"; *identity; continuity*; John 20:1-16).

Thus the images used by Paul in connection with resurrection hope give expression to these two dimensions. Between the seed and the plant, there is *continuity*. One does not get an apple tree from an orange seed. But there is also an aspect of *discontinuity*. There is quite a difference between the decaying and dying seed in the ground and the healthy, full-grown plant or tree!

We would like to know more about the details of death and resurrection and about the nature of the resurrection body. But Paul's "Fool!" (1 Cor 15:36) and the "Who knows?" of Ecclesiastes (3:21) both indicate that in these matters there will remain many things we don't know. There will remain a good deal of mystery. But nonetheless, says Paul, "Death has been swallowed up in victory" (1 Cor 15:54).

4. One of the most eloquent as well as comforting expressions of Christian hope for life after death is to be found at the conclusion of the first half of Paul's letter to the Christians at Rome.
This section begins:

> What then are we to say about these things? If God is for us, who is against us? He who did not withhold his own Son, but gave him up for all of us, will he not with him also give us everything else? (Rom 8:31-32)

It concludes with a ringing declaration of Christian hope for life beyond death. The move from the "Who knows?" of Eccl 3:21 to the "I am convinced" of Paul reflects the apostle's situation on the A.D. side of Christ's resurrection:

> For I am convinced that neither *death,* nor life, nor angels, nor rulers, nor things present, nor things to come, nor powers, nor height, nor depth, nor anything else in all creation, will be able to separate us from the love of God in Christ Jesus our Lord. (Rom 8:38-39, emphasis mine)

To summarize the investigation of Ecclesiastes 6 and 7, in the context of the "story" of the book as a whole: We do hear the *hevel, hevel* theme sounding like a pedal point on an organ through these chapters, in 6:2, 4, 9, 11 (also in 6:12; 7:15 *hevel* is translated "vain"). These texts remind us of the unfairness of life (6:2) and of a judgment that life as a whole can be considered worthless (6:4, 12; 7:15). They also advise us that work can be unsatisfying (6:7) and that too many words can be just so much wind (6:11). We also hear a good deal about death (6:1-6, 12; 7:1-4) in these chapters. Little is said about joy here (only "in the day of prosperity be joyful," recommended in 7:14). One can understand Robinson's comment about the book having the "smell of the tomb" about it (see p. 4 above).

But the story in Ecclesiastes continues, and the parts should be read in the light of the story of the book as a whole. There is more about the limitations of our understanding and the wickedness that exists in the world, and the sounding of the *hevel* theme in chapter 8. However, against this dark background, the "joy" theme resounds again (8:15). That theme will be given its most extensive expression in Ecclesiastes 9, 11, and 12.

7 So How Should I Live My Life?
Ecclesiastes 9, 11, 12

In the world to come, each of us will be called to account for all the good things God put on earth which we refused to enjoy.

The Talmud, cited in Kushner, p. 82

Memento Mori (*Remember that we must die*)

Traditional motto

Carpe Diem (*Seize the day*)

Traditional motto

Now I lay me down to sleep, I pray the Lord my soul to keep.
If I should die before I wake, I pray the Lord my soul to take.

Traditional childhood prayer, the second line of
which is nowadays usually changed to:
"May angels watch me through the night,
and wake me with the morning light."

The first chapter of the book of Ecclesiastes identifies the author as the Teacher (Hebrew *Qoheleth*) three times (1:1, 2, 12), and that identification continues through the middle of the book (7:27) and at the end (12:8, 9, 10). The task of a teacher is to teach, and that teaching often takes the form of *instruction,* with verbs in the imperative mood. One can observe, for example, the book of Proverbs, where the first section consists mainly of instruction, longer essays with verbs in the imperative mood (chs. 1–9). For example, putting the imperative verbs in italics: "*Trust* in the LORD. . . . *Honor* the LORD. . . . *Do* not *despise* the LORD's discipline" (Prov 3:5, 9, 11). The last section of Proverbs is made up of a variety of shorter *sayings* (the bulk of chs. 10–30).

We have noted that the first section of *instruction* in Ecclesiastes, dominated by imperative verbs and with second person address, occurs in 5:1-7, which contains teaching about the hearer's/reader's relationship to God (see Chapter 5 above). Now in chapters 9, 11 and 12 there are more *instruction* sections, with verbs in the imperative, addressing hearers/readers in the second person "you" form. These segments are 9:7-10; 11:9–12:8; and 12:13. Here is advice on how to live, commending the enjoyment of table fellowship ("wine"), marriage ("woman"), and vocation ("work") (9:7-10). As the book winds down, the Teacher lays out some more *instruction* (imperative verbs and "you" address), advising the audience to enjoy life ("rejoice") and to keep the Creator in mind ("remember"; 11:9–12:8) with reverence and obedience ("fear," "keep"; 12:13).

In these final instructional sections, the Teacher is neither reflecting nor reminiscing. The Teacher is teaching. Here is straight-on instruction, eyeball-to-eyeball, and if we wish to hear what this Teacher really has to teach, we do well to listen up!

Memento Mori (Ecclesiastes 9:1-6)

> ¹All this I laid to heart, examining it all, how the righteous and the wise and their deeds are in the hand of God; whether it is love or hate one does not know. Everything that confronts them ²is vanity,

since the same fate comes to all, to the righteous and the wicked, to the good and the evil, to the clean and the unclean, to those who sacrifice and those who do not sacrifice. As are the good, so are the sinners; those who swear are like those who shun an oath. ³This is an evil in all that happens under the sun, that the same fate comes to everyone. Moreover, the hearts of all are full of evil; madness is in their hearts while they live, and after that they go to the dead. ⁴But whoever is joined with all the living has hope, for a living dog is better than a dead lion. ⁵The living know that they will die, but the dead know nothing; they have no more reward, and even the memory of them is lost. ⁶Their love and their hate and their envy have already perished; never again will they have any share in all that happens under the sun.

We have noted in the previous chapter that remembering one's mortality is an important theme in Ecclesiastes (see p. 94 above). Ecclesiastes 9 begins with such a *memento mori* (Latin "remember that we must die") section, advising that one ought not forget that "the same fate comes to all" (9:1-6; see vv. 2, 3). Qoheleth begins this section by acknowledging that everything is in God's hands (v. 1). This does not mean that humans are mere passive puppets, being controlled by some sort of deterministic strings in the hands of a celestial Puppeteer. On the contrary. The Teacher advises students to take life into their own hands, to grab on with all the gusto they've got (v. 10)! The Teacher means to say that humans have been given great freedom in living out their lives and should exercise that freedom joyfully (vv. 7-10), but that God has ultimate control. The old song gets it right, "He's Got the Whole World in His Hands."

Then the Teacher emphasizes that eventually "the same fate comes to all," that is, we all die. Qoheleth names a series of pairs: righteous and wicked, good and evil, clean and unclean, those who sacrifice and those who don't, declaring that all of these die (9:1-3).

But while acknowledging the inevitability of death, this Teacher is radically pro-life, in any form, asserting that even the most humble life, even a dog's life, is to be preferred to death: "a living dog is better than a dead lion." A comment about this saying: in the Bible, dogs are ordinarily viewed as scavengers and are somewhat despised. Thus when Saul sees that David is coming out to fight him, he says to David, "Am I a dog, that you come to me with sticks?" (1 Sam 17:43; see also 1 Sam 24:14; 2 Sam 3:8; 9:8; 16:9 for this same attitude). At the time of Tobit (probably written in the 2nd century B.C.E.), the dog appears as a family pet, who accompanies Tobias on his journey to far-off Rages (Tob 6:1). According to some manuscripts, the dog runs ahead to function as a herald announcing the return of Tobias and the travelers: "And the dog that they had taken along ran ahead, and came as a messenger, wagged his tail, jumped up and demonstrated his joy!" (Tob 11:9, here translating from a contemporary German Bible). The dogs mentioned in Matt 15:21-28 appear to be household pets. The lion, on the other hand, is viewed as a powerful and noble beast (Gen 49:9; Isa 38:13; Job 10:16: "Bold as a lion," etc.).

In any case, 9:1-6 functions as a reminder that all die. This sets the stage for the *instruction* section that follows.

God Wants You to Enjoy! (Ecclesiastes 9:7-10)

> 7Go, eat your bread with enjoyment, and drink your wine with a merry heart; for God has long ago approved what you do. 8Let your garments always be white; do not let oil be lacking on your head. 9Enjoy life with the wife whom you love, all the days of your vain life that are given you under the sun, because that is your portion in life and in your toil at which you toil under the sun. 10Whatever your hand finds to do, do with your might; for there is no work or thought or knowledge or wisdom in Sheol, to which you are going.

Here the Teacher offers some direction on how one ought to live one's life. The imperative verbs in 9:7-10 ("Go, eat . . . drink . . . let be . . . do let . . . enjoy . . . do") mark this as a piece of *instruction,* designed for teaching those who are listening. The literary context for this instruction is important. It follows the *memento mori* section in 9:1-6 and is thus instruction given in full awareness of the reality of human mortality. Children of my generation learned to pray each night, "If I should die before I wake," before falling asleep. And we have also taught our children the same bedtime prayer. Though we children didn't reflect much on it, this prayer was a daily reminder of our mortality. If it is true that one day I will die, then how should I spend each day that I am alive? Verses 7-10 of this chapter offer the longest sequence of imperative verbs, the longest section of *instruction,* in the entire book of Ecclesiastes.

Not only are these imperatives given motivation by the remembering of mortality in verses 1-6, but each of these imperatives is given a reason, in the context of verses 7-10.

Verse 7 counsels enjoying the friendly atmosphere of good table fellowship, here described in terms of the basics, bread and wine: "Go . . . eat . . . drink." This instruction is given a theological endorsement: God approves of what you do! Once again, a section commending enjoyment also speaks of God making connection with humans (see 2:24-26 and related texts, pp. 33-35 above).

The instruction given in verse 8 is suited to the warm climate in Jerusalem: Put on some fresh, light-colored clothing to reflect the heat, and put on some suntan oil to protect your skin! Why? This will make you feel good and add to your enjoyment of life! The mention of oil on the head takes me back to my childhood and youth, when the standard practice of our town barber was to rub a generous supply of Wildroot Cream Oil (or an equivalent) into one's head after a haircut: How sweet it was! Psalm 23:5 refers to the generous hospitality of a host toward a guest saying, "you anoint my head with oil." We may remember also the generosity of the woman who showed hospitality to Jesus by rubbing his feet with oil (Luke 7:46).

Verse 9 provides yet more instruction for living. Husbands and wives are advised to enjoy each day of their lives together, while they can! But how should they do that? Following Ecclesiastes in the Old Testament is the Song of Solomon, which may be understood as spelling out Qoheleth's advice to "enjoy life with the wife whom you love." This seldom-read biblical book is really a handbook for lovers, a marriage manual, a collection of love poetry describing and promoting sexual expression of love between a man and a woman. These pieces do not fit well in the bright light of a classroom, with thoroughly-footnoted discussions of date, setting, forms of poetry, and so on. Like all love poetry, these poems are best read by lovers who are alone with each other, perhaps in the evening by candlelight, accompanied by a glass of wine and an appropriate CD. Here are sample verses, from *The Message* translation by Eugene Peterson. He says to her:

> You're so beautiful, my darling,
>   so beautiful, and your dove eyes are veiled
> By your hair as it flows and shimmers,
>   like a flock of goats in the distance
>   streaming down a hillside in the sunshine.
> Your smile is generous and full —
>   expressive and strong and clean.
> Your lips are jewel red,
>   your mouth elegant and inviting,
>   your veiled cheeks soft and radiant.
> The smooth, lithe lines of your neck
>   command notice — all heads turn in awe and admiration!
> Your breasts are like fawns,
>   twins of a gazelle, grazing among the first spring flowers.
>
> The sweet, fragrant curves of your body,
>   the soft, spiced contours of your flesh
> Invite me, and I come. I stay
>   until dawn breathes its light and night slips away.
> You're beautiful from head to toe, my dear love,
>   beautiful beyond compare, absolutely flawless.
>
>   (4:1-7)

And she says:

My dear lover glows with health —
 red-blooded, radiant!
He's one in a million.
 There's no one quite like him!
My golden one, pure and untarnished,
 with raven black curls tumbling across his shoulders.
His eyes are like doves, soft and bright,
 but deep-set, brimming with meaning, like wells of water.
His face is rugged, his beard smells like sage,
 His voice, his words, warm and reassuring.
Fine muscles ripple beneath his skin,
 quiet and beautiful.
His torso is the work of a sculptor,
 hard and smooth as ivory.
He stands tall, like a cedar,
 strong and deep-rooted,
A rugged mountain of a man,
 aromatic with wood and stone.
His words are kisses, his kisses words.
 Everything about him delights me, thrills me through
  and through!

That's my lover, that's my man,
 dear Jerusalem sisters.

(5:10-16)

Such is the love poetry in the Song of Solomon. Interested readers may continue reading the book on their own, accompanied by appropriate music and wine.

The sense of the instruction given here is similar to the advice given in Sirach 14:14: "Do not deprive yourself of a day's enjoyment; do not let your share of desired good pass by you." Sirach's instruction speaks of a one-day-at-a-time sort of living, enjoying the present while one can, without anxiety about what the future might bring. We are reminded of the Teacher's words about the advantages of life together over life alone (4:9-12).

"All the days of your vain *(hevel)* life" (9:9) sounds the *hevel* theme again. In *The Message,* Eugene Peterson translates *hevel* as "precarious" in this context. His rendering of 9:7-10 catches the sense and the spirit of the whole section well:

> Seize life! Eat bread with gusto,
> Drink wine with a robust heart.
> Oh yes — God takes pleasure in *your* pleasure!
> Dress festively every morning.
> Don't skimp on colors and scarves.
> Relish life with the spouse you love
> Each and every day of your precarious life.
> Each day is God's gift. It's all you get in exchange
> For the hard work of staying alive.
> Make the most of each one!

Finally, verse 10 advises people to throw themselves into their work with enthusiasm, whatever that work may be! The assumption here is that this is enjoyable work. The reason given for working again ties up with the *memento mori* theme: there will be no chance to plant crops, or encounter new ideas, or build houses, or heal patients, or make music, or whatever one's work may be in the world of the dead! Andrew Marvell once wrote:

> The grave's a fine and private place,
> but none, I think, do there embrace.[1]

In reflecting on this section, one is reminded of an expression of the "enjoy" theme, given a reason with a reminder of one's mortality, in the popular song of the 1950s, "Enjoy Yourself! It's Later than You

1. "To His Coy Mistress," in *A Treasury of Great Poems,* edited by Louis Untermeyer (New York: Simon and Schuster, 1942), p. 484.

Think." The second verse of the song gives clear expression to the *memento mori* theme:

You're gonna take that ocean trip, no matter, come what may;
    You've got your reservations made, but you just can't get away.
Next year, for sure, you'll see the world, you'll really get around;
    But how far can you travel when you're six feet under ground?

Then the refrain advises, *carpe diem,* seize the day while you can:

Enjoy yourself, it's later than you think!
    Enjoy yourself, while you're still in the pink.
The years go by, as quickly as a wink,
    Enjoy yourself, enjoy yourself, it's later than you think.[2]

It's a Chancy Kind of Life (Ecclesiastes 9:11-12)

[11]Again I saw that under the sun the race is not to the swift, nor the battle to the strong, nor bread to the wise, nor riches to the intelligent, nor favor to the skillful; but time and chance happen to them all. [12]For no one can anticipate the time of disaster. Like fish taken in a cruel net, and like birds caught in a snare, so mortals are snared at a time of calamity, when it suddenly falls upon them.

That heroic crime fighter of both radio and television fame, Sheriff Matt Dillon, used to introduce each episode of the radio show *Gunsmoke* by saying, "It's a chancy job, and it makes a man watchful." This segment of Ecclesiastes extends that observation, speaking about the chanciness of all human life. But first, a quick look back at Eccl 9:7-10. This advice to enjoy life, not in terms of "wine, women, and song," but rather, "wine, woman, and work," is placed between

2. Herb Magidson, "Enjoy Yourself (It's Later than You Think)," E. H. Morris/ Magidson Music Co. Inc., 1934.

two sections which are reminders that humans are not in complete control of their lives. All humans are subject to the limits of life and the reality of death (9:1-6). And all humans are subject to the fortunes and misfortunes of time and of chance.

Jesus once spoke of 18 persons who were killed in a construction accident in Jerusalem. Why did these people have to die? Jesus provides no answer, other than to say it was not because they were worse sinners than others (Luke 13:4). It was an accident, and as the saying goes, "accidents happen." This is what Qoheleth is saying here, in 9:11: "time and chance happen to them all." The sheriff of Dodge City was right; for all of us, life itself is "a chancy job."

The Teacher rejects some popular assumptions in these two verses. Those whom one would expect to be winners do not always win! The fastest, the strongest, the wisest, the smartest, the most skilled, are all subject to the unpredictable whims of time and chance! And why do such things happen? Even the most intelligent persons can't seem to avoid them, nor can they explain them (8:17).

But the Teacher's counsel remains clear. Living in the midst of the inevitability of death on the one side (9:1-6) and the incalculability, the "chanciness" of events on the other (9:11-12), humans are called to enjoy the good times that they have and the good things that God gives them. We recall the words of the Talmud as cited above: "In the world to come, each of us will be called to account for all the good things God put on earth which we refused to enjoy."

Rejoice, Remember, Revere, and Live Rightly (Ecclesiastes 11:7–12:8, 13)

> **11** ⁷Light is sweet, and it is pleasant for the eyes to see the sun. ⁸Even those who live many years should rejoice in them all; yet let them remember that the days of darkness will be many. All that comes is vanity. ⁹Rejoice, young man, while you are young, and let your heart cheer you in the days of your youth. Follow the inclination of your heart and the desire of your eyes, but know that for all

these things God will bring you into judgment. ¹⁰Banish anxiety from your mind, and put away pain from your body; for youth and the dawn of life are vanity.

12 ¹Remember your creator in the days of your youth, before the days of trouble come, and the years draw near when you will say, "I have no pleasure in them"; ²before the sun and the light and the moon and the stars are darkened and the clouds return with the rain; ³in the day when the guards of the house tremble, and the strong men are bent, and the women who grind cease working because they are few, and those who look through the windows see dimly; ⁴when the doors on the street are shut, and the sound of the grinding is low, and one rises up at the sound of a bird, and all the daughters of song are brought low; ⁵when one is afraid of heights, and terrors are in the road; the almond tree blossoms, the grasshopper drags itself along and desire fails; because all must go to their eternal home, and the mourners will go about the streets; ⁶before the silver cord is snapped, and the golden bowl is broken, and the pitcher is broken at the fountain, and the wheel broken at the cistern, ⁷and the dust returns to the earth as it was, and the breath returns to God who gave it. ⁸Vanity of vanities, says the Teacher; all is vanity. . . . ¹³Fear God, and keep his commandments; for that is the whole duty of everyone.

This last section of the book provides some *instruction*.

How Sweet It Is! (11:7)

Two things in the book of Ecclesiastes are described as "sweet": the sleep of the laborer (5:12) and here, the light of the morning sun (11:7). The Hebrew word translated "sweet" does not occur often in the Bible. It is used in a saying commending the eating of honey: "My child, eat honey, for it is good, and the drippings of the honeycomb are *sweet* to your taste" (Prov 24:13; see also the honey that Samson found, Judg 14:8). Everyone who has put in a hard day's physical work can appreciate this saying about the laborer's sleep! And the "sweetness" of the morning sun? I recall an older friend with whom I spoke regularly, by amateur radio. He would begin almost every day's transmission with the words: "It's a beautiful day here in Denver! How I love to see that sun come up each morning!" Indeed. How sweet it is, to awaken from a good night's sleep and to see the sunshine of another beautiful day!

For Senior Citizens: Rejoice in Each Day! (11:8)

The first "R" in 11:7–12:8 commends daily rejoicing, beginning with those who are older. "Even those who live many years should *rejoice* in them all" (11:8). The Teacher considers this to be good counsel not only for the young people to whom his book is primarily addressed, but also for senior citizens: "Even if you live to a ripe old age you should try to enjoy each day" translates the CEV. How should one "enjoy each day"? Commenting on this text, Ellen Davis speaks of:

> the ability to take pleasure in gifts so small that most of the time we scarcely think of them as gifts. . . . "This is the day that the LORD has made; let us *rejoice* and be glad in it" (Psalm 118:24); the words belong in our daily routine, along with brushing our teeth and getting some physical exercise. Like muscles, the capacity for joy atrophies if we do not use it regularly. Those who wait for some great occasion for joy and gratitude to God are not likely to recognize it when it happens. But from a biblical perspective, lack of humble gratitude leads to loss far more significant than our own unhappiness. For if we fail to take delight every single day, then God will not adequately be praised — and it is quite possible that resounding praise is the whole reason the world was made in the first place.[3] (emphasis mine)

3. Ellen F. Davis, *Proverbs, Ecclesiastes, and the Song of Songs* (Louisville: John Knox, 2000), p. 221.

For Senior Citizens: Remember Your Mortality! (11:8)

The second "R" directed to senior citizens recalls the *memento mori* theme. The matter is stated briefly: "Even those who live many years should rejoice in them all; yet let them *remember* that the days of darkness will be many" (11:8). Another translation: "Even if you live a long time, don't take a single day for granted. Take delight in each light-filled hour" *(The Message)*. In the words of the pop song, "Enjoy yourself, it's later than you think!"

What follows in the remainder of these last chapters of Ecclesiastes is *instruction* directed at young people (11:9; 12:1).

For Young People: Rejoice While You Are Young! (11:9)

Now the same pair of "R's" appears, this time focused on young people. The intended audience is named three times so that the point is not missed: "while you are young" (v. 9) and "in the days of your youth" (11:9; 12:1).

We might have expected the Teacher to lay some imperatives on the young, in the manner of the teachers whose words we find in Proverbs (work hard, get up early, lead a chaste and pure life). Notice some advice from Proverbs, as translated by Eugene Peterson:

You lazy fool, look at an ant.
Watch it closely; let it teach you a thing or two.

(Prov 6:6)

The one who stays on the job has food on the table.

(12:11)

The diligent find freedom in their work;
the lazy are oppressed by work.

(12:24)

Life collapses on loafers;
lazybones go hungry.

(19:15)

> Don't be too fond of sleep; you'll end up in the poorhouse.
>> Wake up and get up; then there'll be food on the table.
>>>> (20:13)

> Just as a door turns on its hinges,
>> so a lazybones turns back over in bed.
>>>> (26:14)

> You can buy an hour with a whore for a loaf of bread,
>> but a wanton woman may well eat *you* alive.
>>>> (6:26)

But Qoheleth does not reel off a string of tired prohibitions for his young audience. Not at all! Here are some more upbeat words for young persons, beginning with: "*Rejoice,* young people, while you are young, and let your heart cheer you in the days of your youth" (v. 9, my translation). Luther comments on this section of Ecclesiastes:

> Solomon is, therefore, the best of teachers of youth. He does not forbid joys and pleasures, as those foolish teachers, the monks, did. For this is nothing else than making young people into stumps and, as even Anselm, the most monkish of monks, said, trying to plant a tree in a narrow pot. So the monks confined their pupils as though in a cage and forbade them to see or talk with people, with the result that they learned and experienced nothing, even though there is nothing more dangerous to youth than solitude. . . . One must see and hear the world, so long as there is a good teacher present. Above all, young people should avoid sadness and loneliness. Joy is as necessary for youth as food and drink, for the body is invigorated by a happy spirit. (*Notes on Ecclesiastes,* pp. 176-77)

For Young People: Remember Your Creator! *(12:1-8)*

This directive to *Remember!* is not aimed at older people, inviting them to review God's guidance and blessing over a long lifetime.

116

These words are directed to the young, "in the days of your youth" (12:1; also 11:9), advising them to enter early on into a habit of *remembering* God every day and to carry out this practice throughout the lifetime that lies ahead of them.

Ecclesiastes 12:1-8 is one of the few examples of an *allegory* in the Bible. The Bible uses a variety of comparative devices. Most well known are *parables,* where Jesus uses true-to-life stories to make a point (Luke 15, for example). The Bible also has a few examples of *fables,* where a "fabulous" or not-true-to-life story is told, to make a point. For an example, note the fable about talking trees in Judg 9:7-21:

> The trees once went out
>   to anoint a king over themselves,
> so they said to the olive tree,
>   "Reign over us."
> The olive tree answered them,
>   "Shall I stop producing my rich oil . . . ?"

Very common in the Bible are *metaphors,* where one reality takes the place of another ("The Lord is my shepherd," Psalm 23). A series of metaphors is called an *allegory,* where a number of realities are used in place of others. Ezekiel 17:3-10 provides a good example of a biblical allegory:

> The word of the LORD came to me; O mortal, propound a riddle, and speak an allegory to the house of Israel. Say: Thus says the Lord GOD:
>
> > A great eagle, with great wings and long pinions,
> >   rich in plumage of many colors,
> >   came to the Lebanon.
> > He took the top of the cedar,
> >   broke off its topmost shoot.
> > He carried it to a land of trade,
> >   set it in a city of merchants.
>
> (Ezek 17:1-4)

117

The key to understanding this allegory: the *great eagle* is Nebuchad-nezzar, king of Babylon; the *topmost shoot* is Judah's King Jehoia-chin, who was taken captive to Babylon, a *city of merchants*. The point is that in an allegory, several terms are used as symbols (great eagle, topmost shoot, city of merchants), each pointing to a reality. The prophet Ezekiel provides a key to interpretation of the text in 17:11-15.

The clue to understanding Eccl 12:1-8 is to recognize that this is an extended allegory, describing the process of aging in terms of the story of an old house that is falling apart! Again, several terms are used as symbols, each pointing to a reality.

Verse 1 indicates that Ecclesiastes is aimed at the young, those who are about 14 or 15 years old, the age for the rite of Confirmation in a number of Christian traditions. In going through some papers that I had stored away, I discovered the church bulletin for the day of my own Confirmation, at age 14, in the Lutheran Church in our town. It was Pentecost 1949, and the bulletin lists the names of 11 young people who were being confirmed that day. On the cover of the bulletin (see p. 119) is the well-known picture of the young boy Jesus in the temple. Under that picture are printed the words of Eccl 12:1-7, with the words "REMEMBER NOW THY CREATOR IN THE DAYS OF THY YOUTH" in capitals, in red. An appropriate text for that day of "Confirmation," which is a rite of passage marking the transition from childhood to becoming a person able to accept adult responsibilities in the life of the church. Whatever editor selected that text for that bulletin cover had the right instincts. As this text indicates clearly, the book of Ecclesiastes is aimed at young people, those just entering into adulthood, here counseling them to *rejoice* and to *remember*. Verse 2 means simply "before death," the time when there is darkness.

With verse 3 the allegory begins, with many elements in the text pointing to an aspect in the life of one growing old. The "guards" refers to the arms, now trembling at the time of old age. The "strong men" refers to the legs, now bowed and bent with age. "The women who grind," who "cease working because they are few," refers to the

REMEMBER NOW THY CREATOR IN THE DAYS OF THY YOUTH, while the evil days come not, nor the years draw nigh, when thou shalt say, I have no pleasure in them; While the sun, or the light, or the moon, or the stars, be not darkened, nor the clouds return after the rain:

In the day when the keepers of the house shall tremble, and the strong men shall bow themselves, and the grinders cease because they are few, and those that look out of the windows be darkened, And the doors shall be shut in the streets, when the sound of the grinding is low, and he shall rise up at the voice of the bird, and all the daughters of musick shall be brought low:

Also when they shall be afraid of that which is high, and fears shall be in the way, and the almond tree shall flourish, and the grasshopper shall be a burden, and desire shall fail: because man goeth to his long home, and the mourners go about the streets: Or ever the silver cord be loosed, or the golden bowl be broken, or the pitcher be broken at the fountain, or the wheel broken at the cistern.

Then shall the dust return to the earth as it was: and the spirit shall return unto God who gave it.

Ecclesiastes 12:1-7

teeth, and "those who look through the windows" is a reference to the eyes. Not a pleasant picture, Qoheleth's imaginative description of old age!

Verse 4 points to senior citizenship as the time to purchase a hearing aid, and also as a time when one wakens early! Older people, says the Teacher in verse 5, are also afraid of heights, presumably, lest they fall and break a hip or an arm! The CEV translation points to further evidences of aging and describes an old person's funeral: "Your hair will turn as white as almond blossoms. You will feel lifeless and drag along like an old grasshopper. We each go to our own eternal home, and the streets are filled with those who mourn."

Finally, this allegory of aging winds down with four pictures of death. Here are four things that are broken: a silver cord, a golden bowl, a pitcher, and a wheel. It is not immediately clear what these items are. It has been suggested that the golden bowl is actually a lamp suspended from a silver cord. The pitcher and wheel could be utensils used for drawing water from a cistern or well. Perhaps these broken items are symptoms of an estate going to ruin. In any case, taken together, these four symbolize loss of function and brokenness. And immediately following is a declaration of loss of human function and of brokenness, "the dust returns to the earth." The word *dust* here links up with the same word used in the creation story in Gen 2:7: "then the LORD God formed man from the *dust* of the ground," and also in the Bible's earliest declaration of human mortality, "You are *dust,* and to *dust* you shall return" in Gen 3:19. These *dust* words declaring the end of human life are familiar from the funeral liturgy in a number of churches, accompanying the throwing or shoveling of soil onto the casket in the grave.

Ecclesiastes continues, "and the spirit (Hebrew *ruach*) returns to God who gave it" (v. 7). The Hebrew word is translated in a variety of ways: "And the *lifebreath* returns to God" (JPS); "and the *life-giving breath* returns to God" (CEV); "and the *breath of life* will go back to God, who gave it to us" (TEV).

The closing "vanity of vanities" in 12:8 links with 1:2, thus tying the book together. And then, like an explanatory addition to a movie or DVD, the book concludes with an Epilogue, which will be discussed in Chapter 8 below.

For Both Young and Old: Revere God and Live Rightly! (12:13)

The third imperative in these chapters comes at the end of the book and is now addressed to all readers and hearers. After having been instructed to *rejoice* and to *remember* their Creator, both senior citizens and teenagers are advised to "*Revere* God and observe His commandments" (JPS). The Hebrew/Jewish tradition in reading the ending of Ecclesiastes is to read verse 13 a second time, after verse 14, in order to avoid ending the book on a negative note (see the JPS translation) and to emphasize this final instruction to *revere* God and to "keep God's commandments," that is, to *live rightly.* Thus the book of Ecclesiastes and the "story" that runs through it come to a conclusion with some easily remembered advice and some practical instruction, for young and old alike: *Rejoice* while you are young! *Remember* your Creator while you are young! *Revere* God! And *Live Rightly,* letting God's commandments be your guide.

To summarize the material from Ecclesiastes 9, 11 and 12: The pedal note, *hevel,* continues to drone on in these last chapters, in connection with the inevitability of death (9:12), the coming of dark days (11:8), and even in describing the time of youth (11:10). It is sounded for the final time after the description of dying and death in 12:2-7: "*hevel, hevel,* all is *hevel*" (12:8), linking up with the same theme at the beginning of the book (1:2). This *hevel* theme, however, is not the dominant note in these final chapters of the book of Ecclesiastes. Even in this context of the inevitability of death and the incalculability of chance (9:11-12), the Teacher instructs hearers, both old and young, to *remember* and to *revere* their Creator (11:8; 12:1, 13), and especially and emphatically to *rejoice* (9:7-10; 11:8-9).

Succoth, the Festival for Rejoicing

Among the three major feasts celebrated in ancient Israel was Succoth, or the Festival of Booths (Deut. 16:1-17 lists these festivals: Unleavened Bread or Passover, Weeks, Booths or Succoth). The tone of the ancient harvest festival was one of joy. Note the directions for celebrating in Deut 16:13-15:

> You shall keep the festival of booths (Hebrew *sukkoth*) for seven days, when you have gathered in the produce from your threshing floor and your wine press. *Rejoice* during your festival, you and your sons and your daughters, your male and female slaves, as well as the Levites, the strangers, the orphans, and the widows resident in your towns. Seven days you shall keep the festival for the LORD your God at the place that the LORD will choose; for the LORD your God will bless you in all your produce and in all your undertakings, and you shall surely celebrate. (emphasis mine; see also Zech 14:16-19; 2 Chr 8:13; Lev 23:34)

Sukkoth continues to be one of the major festivals celebrated by present-day Jews. That celebration includes the building of a small temporary structure called a *sukkah,* a place for eating and drinking and visiting with family and friends. Rabbi Kushner describes this time of joy:

> In the Jewish tradition, we celebrate a holiday every autumn known as Sukkot, the Feast of Tabernacles. It is, in part, an old harvest festival, deriving from a time when the Israelites were farmers and would give thanks every autumn when the harvest had been gathered. In fact, it is the prototype of our American festival of Thanksgiving. And, in part, it is a commemoration of God's protecting care over Israel during the forty years in the wilderness between Egypt and the Promised Land.
>
> We celebrate Sukkot by building a small annex to our homes, just a few boards and branches, inviting friends in, and drinking

wine and eating fruit in it for the week of the holiday. Sukkot is a celebration of the beauty of things that don't last, the little hut which is so vulnerable to wind and rain (ours regularly collapses a day or two after we put it up) and will be dismantled at week's end; the ripe fruits which will spoil if not picked and eaten right away; the friends who may not be with us for as long as we would wish; and in northern climates, the beauty of the leaves changing color as they begin the process of dying and falling from the trees. Sukkot comes in the fall. Summer is over and sometimes the evenings are already chilly with the first whispers of winter. It comes to tell us that the world is full of good and beautiful things, food and wine, flowers and sunsets and autumn landscapes and good company to share them with, but that we have to enjoy them right away because they will not last. They will not wait for us to finish other things and get around to them. It is a time to "eat our bread in gladness and drink our wine with joy" [Ecclesiastes 9:7], not despite the fact that life does not go on forever but precisely because of that fact. It is a time to enjoy happiness with those we love and to realize that we are at a time in our lives when enjoying today means more than worrying about tomorrow. It is a time to celebrate the fact that we have finally learned what life is about and how to make the most of it. The special scriptural reading assigned for study in the synagogue during the Feast of Tabernacles is the Book of Ecclesiastes.[4]

---

4. Harold Kushner, *When All You've Ever Wanted Isn't Enough* (New York: Summit, 1986), pp. 189-90.

8 What It's All About
Ecclesiastes for Our Time

The great doubter? No! Qoheleth was the great believer. He believed, when there was no evidence for believing!

> Roland Murphy at a break in a meeting of the
> Society of Biblical Literature, in response to
> a question about Ecclesiastes

Emily, through her tears, asks the stage manager:
*Do any human beings ever realize life while they live it? —
    every, every minute?*
He replies:
No. [Pause] The saints and poets, maybe — they do some.

> Thorton Wilder, "Our Town," Act III

Count it all joy, my brothers and sisters.

> Jas 1:2

The End of the Matter (Ecclesiastes 12:9-14)

⁹Besides being wise, the Teacher also taught the people knowledge, weighing and studying and arranging many proverbs. ¹⁰The

Teacher sought to find pleasing words, and he wrote words of truth plainly.

¹¹The sayings of the wise are like goads, and like nails firmly fixed are the collected sayings that are given by one shepherd. ¹²Of anything beyond these, my child, beware. Of making many books there is no end, and much study is a weariness of the flesh.

¹³The end of the matter; all has been heard. Fear God, and keep his commandments; for that is the whole duty of everyone. ¹⁴For God will bring every deed into judgment, including every secret thing, whether good or evil.

In the first part of this chapter (12:1-8) the one speaking is the Teacher: "Vanity of vanities, says the Teacher" (v. 8). Now, beginning with verse 9, the biblical text speaks *about* the Teacher, which leads us to conclude that 12:9-14 is a final word from the editor of the entire book. This ending section thus ties up with 1:1, where once again the editor speaks *about* the Teacher. Certain older commentaries saw the fact that verses 9-14 come from an editor as a negative thing. These are not the words of Qoheleth, they observed, and thus these words are of less value and should be tossed out, like the husks on an ear of corn. But, looked at from a more positive viewpoint, these last sentences from the final editor of the book (NRSV labels vv. 9-14 as an "Epilogue") can be helpful in providing a summary of what has gone on before and in providing further clues to the understanding of the whole book.

The sentences of verses 9-10 take us into the workshop where the Teacher has produced this product, giving us a picture of Qoheleth at work at his desk. Note what is said here:

(1) The Teacher is described as *wise* (v. 9). In the world of the Old Testament there were three categories of leaders; Jeremiah 18:18 lists them: "instruction shall not perish from the *priest,* nor counsel from the *wise,* nor the word from the *prophet.*" The priests were responsible for liturgical activities duties at the place of worship, but also had teaching responsibilities: "For with you is my contention, O priest. . . . My people are destroyed for lack of knowledge. . . . And

since you have forgotten the teaching of your God, I also will forget your children " (Hos 4:4-6, my translation). Prophets were those who brought a message from God, typically beginning their speeches with "Thus says the LORD": "Thus says the LORD: for three transgressions of Damascus, and for four, I will not revoke the punishment" (Amos 1:3; see also 1:6–2:16). And "the wise," which could include men and women (see 2 Sam 14:2; 20:16), offered counsel and advice, such as we find in the biblical books of Proverbs (advice for young people on growing up), Job (thoughts on why good people experience bad things), and certain "wisdom Psalms" (Pss 1, 49, 73, 119).

We know that in any community there are certain people who are natural sympathizers and advisers. They don't have to have academic degrees in psychology, but they do have certain gifts for listening and giving counsel. In the biblical world these persons were called "the wise." Qoheleth is identified as such a person.

(2) Qoheleth is described as *one who teaches:* "Qoheleth [NRSV footnote] also taught the people knowledge" (v. 9). It is possible for a person who is wise to be something of a consultant, a guru, to whom people come for advice. Or a wise person may write learned books, alone in his or her study. But this teacher is here described as engaged in classroom activity. We can imagine a busy house of study, a schoolroom buzzing with students engaged in exchange with the teacher and with one another. The second century B.C.E. writer and teacher Sirach refers to such a place: "Draw near to me, you who are uneducated, and lodge in the house of instruction" (Sir 51:23).

(3) The Teacher engages in *research and study.* Qoheleth is not portrayed as a free-wheeling know-it-all who spontaneously spews advice and counsel from the top of the head. What is described here is hard intellectual work, preparing for classes, in this case evaluating and editing what earlier wise teachers had said. The object of study is "proverbs." The Hebrew word is *meshalim,* which is used in the Hebrew Bible as the title of the Old Testament book of Proverbs.

These two verses nicely describe the work of the teacher, even to this day. First, the one who is going to teach must have some sort of natural talent for the job and must be recognized as one who has at least a measure of wisdom. Second, the teacher must spend some time in preparation, "studying and arranging" (v. 9). Then the teacher has to think about effective pedagogical techniques and devices. The teacher's presentation should then consist of "pleasing words." Attending these classes ought to be a pleasant experience! However, the teaching should not only be pleasant and the class sessions fun. The teacher should be teaching words of *truth* (v. 10)! The CEV translation catches the sense nicely, "Then I tried to explain these things in the best and most accurate way."

Verses 11-12 refer to the wisdom materials that the Teacher studies. The Teacher accommodates his instruction to those being taught. Apparently Qoheleth is working in an agricultural community, where people know about special prods used to get cattle to move. Students need some prodding, too! The point is that instruction is not just an intellectual matter. It ought to result in getting people to change their lives! The sense of "nails firmly fixed" probably means that there are certain sayings, teachings, that you can "hang your hat on" — that is, things that are like axioms in mathematics, things that are "most certainly true," such as "The fear of the LORD is the beginning of wisdom" (Ps 111:10). It would appear that "one shepherd," again an agricultural metaphor, is a reference to God as the source of true wisdom. The CEV translates, "These sayings come from God, our only shepherd."

Verse 12 begins with a warning to stay away from false, heretical teachings that have been around, it would appear, as long as there have been teachers! And then there is the well-known statement, "Of making many books there is no end, and much study is a weariness of the flesh." What would Qoheleth say were he able to step into one of our gigantic bookstores, or attend the Frankfurt Book Fair in Germany, or survey the publications available through the Internet? And "weariness"? Indeed, studying is hard work! Who knows how many students have posted the words "much study is a weariness of the flesh" over their dormitory desks!

The Hebrew word translated "study" here is *lahag*. The same *hag*-root also occurs in Ps 1:2 and is usually translated as "meditate," the

English word calling to mind the picture of a person sitting quietly, hands folded, piously reflecting on deep subjects. However, the same Hebrew word is used to refer to the growling of a lion, just before eating its prey (Isa 31:4). This indicates that the sort of "study" described here and the "meditating" in Ps 1:2 involved reading aloud. The "house of instruction" (Sir 51:23) was no doubt a busy, buzzing place!

"The end of the matter," says verse 13, and the book of Ecclesiastes comes to a close. As a good teacher, the final editor of the book now summarizes the whole thing in just a few words, "while standing on one foot," as the rabbis liked to say: "Revere God, and keep God's commandments!" This is to say: religion has to do with God, and with the neighbor, since the Ten Commandments, for example, are concerned with one's relationship to God (Exod 20:2-11) and to the neighbor (Exod 20:12-17). And then says the Teacher, translating the Hebrew literally, "This is everything for humans." The CEV translates nicely, "This is what life is all about."

The word about judgment in verse 14 has something of a fearsome ring, with the prospect of God settling all scores and discovering every secret wrongdoing. For this reason, Jewish tradition directs that in reading Ecclesiastes publicly verse 13 should be repeated, so that everything ends on a positive note (the JPS translation reflects this practice).[1] Again, the CEV translation is on target: "Everything you were taught can be put into a few words: Respect and obey God! This is what life is all about."

Ecclesiastes and the New Testament

There is only one direct quotation of Ecclesiastes in the New Testament. Romans 3:10, "There is no one who is righteous, not even one," appears to be citing Eccl 7:20. There are, however, a number of places in the New Testament where themes from Ecclesiastes are sounded. I list the following as worth reflecting upon:

---

1. Robert Gordis, *Koheleth* (New York: Schocken, 1968), p. 355.

1. The *rejoice* and *enjoy* theme of Qoheleth (see pp. 135-37 below) finds parallels in the New Testament in the accounts of the joy of the birth of Jesus (Luke 1:14), at the finding of the lost (Luke 15:5, 9, 22-23), and at the resurrection (Matt 28:8; Luke 24:41, 52; John 20:20). Paul's letter to Christians in Philippi is something of an ode to joy. The apostle expresses joy because of the people themselves (Phil 1:4; 4:1, 10), because of the spread of the Gospel (1:12-18), the healing of Epaphroditus (2:25-30), and a general "joy in the Lord" (4:4 twice, 10). Note also "Count it all joy" of Jas 1:2, and 1 Pet 1:6, "In this you rejoice"; 1:8, "and even though you do not see him now, you believe in him and rejoice with an indescribable and glorious joy"; and 4:13, "But rejoice insofar as you are sharing Christ's sufferings, so that you may also be glad and shout for joy when his glory is revealed." The call to rejoice in the New Testament has a new reason for rejoicing: the resurrection of Jesus Christ.

2. While there are traces of an "anti-worldliness" in the New Testament (Jas 1:27; 4:4; 1 John 2:15-17; 5:19), the New Testament, like Qoheleth, also affirms the *goodness of creation,* the *giftedness* of God's people ("all things are yours," 1 Cor 3:21; Matt 6:25-34; Luke 12:22-34) and the joy of an abundant life, now in relationship to Christ (John 10:10).

3. The *"agnosticism about the future"* theme has been identified as one of Qoheleth's major frustrations (see p. 133 below). Jesus has something to say on this matter, counseling against worrying about the future, since believers have a heavenly Father who cares about them (Matt 6:25-34). Using the typical rabbinic "how much more" kind of argument, Jesus illustrated his views about the future by pointing to the lilies of the field and the birds of the air and concluded, "So do not worry about tomorrow" (Matt 6:34; 10:29-31; see also Luke 12:22-34).

Like Qoheleth, the New Testament recognizes that the future is uncertain, but is content to leave that future in the hands of a loving Lord.

And now I have a word for you who brashly announce, "Today — at the latest, tomorrow — we're off to such and such a city for the year.

We're going to start a business and make a lot of money." You don't know the first thing about tomorrow. You're nothing but a wisp of fog, catching a brief bit of sun before disappearing. Instead, make it a habit to say, "If the Master wills it and we're still alive, we'll do this or that." (Jas 4:13-15, *The Message*)

The Apostle Paul has the same attitude toward the future: "But I will come to you soon, *if the Lord wills*" (1 Cor. 4:19), "for I hope to spend some time with you, *if the Lord permits*" (16:7).

4. The *concern for the poor* theme (see p. 133 below) is often articulated in the New Testament. A few examples from many include Matt 19:21; Mark 12:42-43; 14:7; Rom 15:26; Gal 2:10; Jas 2:1-7.

5. If the *faith without sight* theme is important in Ecclesiastes (see pp. 133-34 below), then it is certainly very important in the New Testament as well: "Now faith is the assurance of things hoped for, the conviction of things not seen," Heb 11:1; see also Matt 8:5-13; 15:21-28.

6. The *memento mori (remember that we will all die)* theme that runs through Ecclesiastes (see p. 134 below) is transformed into a new key in the New Testament. "Remember that we must die" is now "Remember that we will live!" Handel's setting of Paul's words about resurrection from 1 Cor 15:51-57 puts it most dramatically:

Behold, I tell you a mystery; we shall not all sleep, but we shall be chang'd in a moment, in the twinkling of an eye, at the last trumpet. The trumpet shall sound, and the dead shall be raised incorruptible. ("The Messiah," Recitative for Bass No. 47, followed by Air for Bass with Trumpet, No. 48)

The Good News that Christ has been raised from the dead and that death has lost its sting (1 Cor 15:55) is central to the *kerygma* or fundamental proclamation of the earliest church. It is the basis for the individual believer's hope for resurrection (1 Cor 15; Rom 8:31-38).

7. Ecclesiastes issues a call to *remember your creator* (12:1; see p. 135 below), thus calling for a remembering of God's act of creation. The New Testament, assuming that the creating work of God has been

sufficiently dealt with in Genesis, the Psalms, and other texts, now calls for remembering the *delivering, saving* work of God. In the action of the celebration of the Lord's Supper Jesus said, "Do this *in remembrance* of me." Since this was a Passover meal, the focus was on remembering and re-enacting God's deliverance of Israel in the events of the Exodus. But now the object of the remembering is God's acts of deliverance from "sin, death and the devil" in the life and work of Jesus Christ (1 Cor 11:25 and context; Luke 22:19 and context).

8. The *importance of community, of life together* theme appears in Ecclesiastes, in the paragraph dealing with the "two are better than one" theme (4:9-12) and in the section about worship, which assumes that the community gathers for worship (5:1-2; see Chapters 4 and 5 above). In the New Testament, the book of Acts reports the rapid growth of the new Christian community (Acts 2:42-47; 4:32-37; 5:12-16) and its gathering for study, the Lord's Supper, and prayer (2:42) and table fellowship and praise (2:46-47). It was in fact said of these early Christians, "see how they love one another" (Tertullian *Apology* 39). Paul's letters to these young churches provide a picture of both the joys and the strains of life together in this new community.

9. Other themes are sounded in Ecclesiastes which are picked up in the New Testament. We name only two here, without developing them further: (1) *work* as a gift to be enjoyed (2:24; 3:13; 5:18) and pursued with vigor (9:10); in the New Testament, Jesus works as a carpenter's son (Matt 13:55) and Paul makes tents (Acts 18:1-3); (2) the dangers of the *love of money* (4:7-8; 5:10); the New Testament tells the stories of the rich young ruler who couldn't part with his money (Mark 10:17-22), of the greed and duplicity of Annas and Sapphira (Acts 5:1-11), and identifies the love of money as the root of evil (1 Tim 6:10).

In any case, it is clear that the book of Ecclesiastes is not an oddity, some sort of embarrassment, in the context of the literature of either the Old or the New Testament. Qoheleth stands firmly as a unique and important voice in the biblical company of believers, though his tent is pitched, as has been suggested, near the edge of the camp.

What It's All About: Ecclesiastes For Our Time

"Soph dabar," says the Hebrew of Eccl 12:13, which means "the end of the matter." The Hebrew word *soph* is used in the expression *"soph pasuk,"* which denotes the punctuation mark at the end of a Hebrew sentence. Thus we could translate this sentence, "Everything has been said. Period!" So what is it all about? We began by speaking of "Getting into Ecclesiastes" (Chapter 1). Now the question is, What can we "get out" of this biblical book that is of importance for our own lives? Why is the book in the biblical canon at all? What follows is a series of suggestions about the importance of Ecclesiastes for our time at the beginning of the 21st century.

1. The book of Ecclesiastes does not express the central message of the biblical faith. The mark of sects or heretical groups claiming the Bible as authority is that they miss the central point of the biblical message. Thus certain groups concentrate their major attention on the book of Revelation and are preoccupied with predicting the end of the world. Other communities may put their emphasis on those parts of the Bible that tell about speaking in tongues, and that activity becomes the center of their religion. And there are also groups for whom the center appears to be what the Bible says about handling poisonous snakes (Mark 16:17-18).

For evangelical Christians, the central focus of the biblical message is expressed in the text that Sunday School pupils learn early on, John 3:16: "For God so loved the world that he gave his only Son, so that everyone who believes in him may not perish but may have eternal life." This text expresses the Gospel, the "evangel," the Good News about what God has done in Christ, that is at the center of the Christian faith.

Where, then, does the book of Ecclesiastes fit in? Someone once wrote that the writer of Ecclesiastes has "pitched his tent at the far edges of the camp," meaning that while the writer of this book is within the company of biblical writers, the message of the book is a bit far out, on the extreme edges of ordinary biblical teachings.

In any case, Ecclesiastes is present in both the Jewish and the

Christian Bible and therefore claims the attention of those who call themselves Jews or Christians.

2. Placed in the context of the Old Testament as a whole, Ecclesiastes should be understood as articulating the response of a wisdom teacher to the words and the acts of God. Somewhat oversimplified, the writings of the Old Testament may be grouped as follows:

(1) The Historical books, which report *what God has done,* including Genesis through Numbers, the Deuteronomistic History (Deuteronomy through 2 Kings, minus Ruth), and the Chronicler's history (1 and 2 Chronicles, Ezra, Nehemiah). The focus in these books is on the *acts of God.*

(2) The Prophetic books, which tell *what God has said,* including Isaiah, Jeremiah, Ezekiel, and the book of the 12 Minor Prophets. The focus in these books is on the *words of God.*

(3) The Psalms and Wisdom literature, which offer *the people's response* to the acts and words of God. Included in this category are books which articulate:

(a) The *response* in praise and lament (the Psalms)

(b) The *response* in reflection and instruction (wisdom literature, including Job, certain Psalms, Proverbs, and Ecclesiastes)

It is helpful to understand the book of Ecclesiastes as one expression of a believer's response to the words and acts of God. For further discussion along these lines, the reader is referred to the Old Testament theologies of both Gerhard von Rad and Claus Westermann (see the Bibliography).

3. The underlying theme for the entire book is struck in 1:2: "Vanity of vanities, all is vanity." The Hebrew word translated "vanity" is *hevel,* the literal meaning for which is "a breath of air, a puff of wind." It signifies something that is without substance, something that appears and then quickly disappears. We have noted that it can be translated as senseless, meaningless, breath of air, smoke, and the like (see pp. 11-13 above). Von Rad has suggested that the word *hevel* runs through Ecclesiastes as a pedal point, a sustained,

supporting bass note on an organ. Thus everything that is said in the book of Ecclesiastes should be heard in relation to that underlying pedal note: "all is *hevel,* a puff of wind, without substance and without permanence."

4. There is a refreshing honesty in Qoheleth's tendency toward agnosticism (ch. 3). The Teacher does not pretend to have all the answers to life's questions. He owns up to mystery: "Just as you do not know how the breath comes to the bones in the mother's womb, so you do not know the work of God, who makes everything" (11:5). His "Who knows?" of 3:21 leaves the matter of life beyond death as a question. A number of passages suggest that the matter of the future is also a nagging question for the Teacher (3:11; 6:12; 7:14; 8:7; 9:12; 10:14; 11:1-6). In the New Testament, the writer of James also admits to not knowing about the future: "Yet you do not even know what tomorrow will bring" (Jas 4:14).

5. There is a social sensitivity behind Qoheleth's attitude toward the poor and the hurting (chs. 4, 5). The Teacher does not live in an ivory tower, but is quite aware of the plight of the oppressed and the hurting in his environment (4:1-3; 5:8-9, 13-17). It is not his task, however, to call for restoring social justice in the community. For guidance on these matters, we could imagine the Teacher saying, "Review what the prophets Amos, Isaiah, and Micah have to say on these issues!"

6. There is a certain heroic quality about Qoheleth's faith and trust in God (ch. 5). Hebrews 11 defines faith as "to be sure of the things we hope for, to be certain of the things we cannot see." Qoheleth didn't *see* much reason for believing and trusting in God. To one living in the third century B.C.E., the stories about God's calling the ancestors, or delivering them out of Egypt, or guiding them through the wilderness, or giving them a land, or prospering the kingdoms of David and Solomon must have seemed ancient and remote. In the glory days of David and Solomon, Israel was indeed the ranking nation in that part of the Mediterranean world. But now, at the time of Qoheleth, the Jews were but a small island in the midst of the vast Greek empire. "God may have been acting then," many Jews must have thought, "but God doesn't seem to be doing much right now!"

God had indeed spoken mightily through the great prophets, like Isaiah, Jeremiah, Ezekiel, and all the rest, in the past. But there were also times when there was no word from God (Ps 74:9), and the time of Qoheleth seems to have been such a time. "God may have spoken then, but God isn't saying much now!" seems to have been the mood of the people. There was indeed a God who ought to be worshipped (Eccl 5), but no one, not even the professional theologians, could tell what God was currently up to (3:11; 6:12; 7:14; 8:17; 11:5).

Nevertheless, Qoheleth did not counsel giving up on God. And Qoheleth still believes, without seeing evidence for that belief. I recall a conversation with the late Professor Roland Murphy, a great interpreter of the Old Testament Wisdom literature. I was teaching through Ecclesiastes for the first time, to a group of college students, and sought out Father Murphy for some conversation during a break at one of the national meetings of the Society of Biblical Literature. I said to him, "Professor Murphy, the writer of Ecclesiastes has often been referred to as a great doubter. What do you think?" His response was immediate and enthusiastic. With excitement and gesturing with both hands, he said, "The great doubter? No! Qoheleth was the great believer! He believed, even when there was no evidence for believing!" Professor Murphy was right, of course, and I have cited his response to students ever since.

7. There is a hardy realism in Qoheleth's attitude toward death (ch. 6). The fool is the one who says "there is no God," according to Psalm 14. The fool is also the one who forgets that he or she is mortal (Luke 12:13-21). Attending a funeral can be a reminder that we are finite creatures, here for a limited time only (Eccl 7:2). The *memento mori* (remember you must die) theme is not the last word. It should be coupled with the *carpe diem* (seize the day) and the *rejoice* themes, according to Qoheleth.

8. A series of imperative verbs express the central points this Teacher is making, always with the *hevel* theme droning in the background: Rejoice, Remember, Revere, and Keep! We shall consider them here in reverse order:

a. *Revere* God and live rightly, according to God's commandments.

135

The NRSV translates "Fear God," which denotes an attitude of re-spect and reverence. I prefer to translate as "revere," with the JPS translation, both for accuracy and for the teacher's mnemonic device of alliteration! The "fear/revere" theme runs through the book: 3:14 (NRSV "awe"); 5:7; 7:18; 8:12, 13; 12:13. The final imperative in the book is *keep* his commandments." For the sake of alliteration, with another "r" word, one could understand this as "live rightly." Since so many of the commandments, the last seven of the Decalogue, re-fer to relationships to other people, these final imperatives in the book nicely summarize the expected response of believers toward God and toward the neighbor.

b. *Remember* your Creator when you are young! The final advice in the book, in 12:1-8, is addressed to young people. Here are no words about working hard, saving money, disciplining oneself in sexual and other affairs, such as one might find in the book of Proverbs. The directive here is simply to "Remember!" The Teacher does not play upon the usual themes at the core of the Old Testament faith, re-membering the mighty acts of God in the calling of the ancestors, the deliverance from Egypt, the giving of the commandments, the guidance in the wilderness, or the conquest of the land. The call to "remember" here focuses on only one aspect of God's work: God the Creator (see also 1:2-11; 3:10-15 for the creating work of God). This is not sufficient for a full-blown biblical theology, but especially for young people it is a good place to begin. The Bible itself, of course, begins by speaking of God the Creator (Genesis. 1, 2).

c. *Rejoice,* old and young alike, enjoying the gifts God has given you! Running through the entire book of Ecclesiastes is a series of seven calls to enjoy life and rejoice in the good gifts God has given: 2:24-26; 3:12-13, 22; 5:18-20; 8:15; 9:7-10; 11:8–12:1 (see Chapters 2 and 7 above). These calls to rejoice are addressed to senior citizens (11:8) as well as to young people (12:1). It is in these passages that one hears about God, as the giver of gifts that make life a joy. Both Luther and Bonhoeffer have called special attention to this "joy" theme in Eccle-siastes (see Chapters 1 and 3 above).

This "rejoice!" theme has been kept alive in Judaism, since Ecclesiastes has been the book to read at the joy-filled fall festival of Sukkot (see Chapter 7 above). In fact, Jewish scholar Robert Gordis states that "joy" is the basic theme of Ecclesiastes:

> That the basic theme of the book was *simḥah,* the enjoyment of life, was clearly recognized by Jewish religious authorities who thus explained the custom of reading *Koheleth* in the synagogue on the Feast of Tabernacles, the Season of Rejoicing.[2]

It is true that *hevel, hevel* sounds throughout the book like a pedal point on an organ. But while important, the pedal point, the sustained note in the bass, is never the main focus of the musical composition. Over against the pedal point, in full awareness of it, there is a melody, perhaps a sturdy chorale, or maybe even an exciting, even joyful counterpoint. I suggest that this counterpoint, the "joy" theme in Ecclesiastes, is really what it is all about. A New Testament writer who does have affinities with the wisdom tradition, started out his letter in a manner which could summarize the theme of Ecclesiastes: "Count it all joy, my brothers and sisters" (Jas 1:2).

In conclusion, a comment on the book as a whole from Luther's commentary:

> To reiterate, the point and the purpose of this book is to instruct us, so that with thanksgiving we may use the things that are present and the creatures of God that are generously given to us and conferred upon us by the blessing of God. This we are to do with-

---

2. Gordis continues, "But whatever the motives that led to the preservation of the book, we cannot be too grateful"; *Koheleth* (New York: Schocken, 1968), p. 131. Gordis cites rabbinic authorities in support of his assertion that the theme is the enjoyment of life: Isaac Tirna, *Sefer Minhagim* (Warsaw, 1882), *Comments on Sukkot,* p. 21b: "The reason seems to me to be that Sukkot is the season of our rejoicing and the book of Koheleth praises joy"; *Magen Abraham, Hilkhot Pesah,* sec. 490, par. 8: "And on Sukkot, *Koheleth* is read, because they are days of joy"; *Lebush, Hilkhot Lulav,* 663: "Succot is the season of our rejoicing and the book of Koheleth praises and encourages men to rejoice in their portion"; Gordis, p. 378, n. 4.

out anxiety about the things that are still in the future. The important thing is that we have a tranquil and quiet heart and a mind filled with joy, that is, that we be content with the Word and work of God. Thus in the verses that follow he exhorts us (9:7-9) to eat and drink and enjoy life with the wife of our youth. . . . This is in accord with the saying of Christ (Matt. 6:34: "The day's own trouble is sufficient for the day"). (*Notes on Ecclesiastes,* p. 10)

Bibliography of Works Cited

Barth, Karl. *Dogmatics in Outline*. Trans. G. T. Thompson. London: SCM, 1958.

Bethge, Eberhard. *Dietrich Bonhoeffer: Eine Biographie*. Munich: Chr. Kaiser, 1967.

———. *Dietrich Bonhoeffer: A Biography*. Translated by Eric Mosbacher. Edited by Edwin Robertson. Rev. ed. Minneapolis: Fortress, 2000.

Bickerman, Elias J. *Four Strange Books of the Bible*. New York: Schocken, 1967.

Bonhoeffer, Dietrich. *Ethics*. Translated by Neville Horton Smith. Edited by Eberhard Bethge. New York: Macmillan, 1955.

———. *Letters and Papers from Prison*. Translated by Reginald H. Fuller and Frank Clarke. Edited by Eberhard Bethge. New York: Macmillan, 1972.

———. *Life Together; Prayerbook of the Bible*. Translated by Donald W. Bloesch and James H. Burtness. Edited by Geoffrey B. Kelly. Vol. 5 of Dietrich Bonhoeffer, *Works,* edited by Gerhard Ludwig Müller and Albrecht Schönherr. Minneapolis: Fortress, 1996.

Brown, William P. *Ecclesiastes*. Interpretation. Louisville: John Knox, 2000.

Davis, Ellen F. *Proverbs, Ecclesiastes, and the Song of Songs*. Westminster Bible Companion. Louisville: Westminster John Knox, 2000.

Dummelow, J. R., ed. *A Commentary on the Holy Bible.* New York: Macmillan, 1952.

Fox, Michael V. *A Time to Tear Down and a Time to Build Up.* Grand Rapids: Wm. B. Eerdmans, 1999.

Ginsburg, Christian D. *The Song of Songs and Coheleth.* New York: Ktav, 1970.

Gordis, Robert. *Koheleth: The Man and His World.* 3rd ed. New York: Schocken, 1968.

Horne, Milton P. *Proverbs, Ecclesiastes.* Smyth & Helwys Bible Commentary. Macon: Smyth & Helwys, 2003.

Krüger, Thomas. *Kohelet.* Biblischer Kommentar Altes Testament XIX (Sonderband). Neukirchen: Neukirchener, 2000.

———. *Qoheleth: A Commentary.* Translated by O. C. Dean, Jr. Edited by Klaus Baltzer. Hermeneia. Minneapolis: Fortress, 2004.

Kushner, Harold. *When All You've Ever Wanted Isn't Enough: The Search for a Life That Matters.* New York: Summit, 1986.

Limburg, James. *The Prophets and the Powerless.* Atlanta: John Knox, 1977; Lima: Academic Renewal, 2001.

Lohfink, Norbert. *Qoheleth.* Continental Commentaries. Translated by Sean McEvenue. Minneapolis: Fortress, 2003.

Luther, Martin. *Luther's Small Catechism.* Translated by Timothy J. Wengert. Minneapolis: Augsburg Fortress, 1994.

———. *Notes on Ecclesiastes.* Luther's Works 15. Edited by Jaroslav Pelikan. St. Louis: Concordia, 1972.

Murphy, Roland. *Ecclesiastes.* Word Biblical Commentary 23A. Waco: Word, 1992.

———. "The Faith of Qoheleth." *Word and World* 7 (1987): 253-60.

———. *Wisdom Literature.* Forms of the Old Testament Literature 13. Grand Rapids: Wm. B. Eerdmans, 1981.

Péguy, Charles. *Basic Verities.* Translated by Ann and Julia Green. New York: Pantheon, 1943.

Peterson, Eugene H. *The Message: The Bible in Contemporary Language.* Colorado Springs: NavPress, 2003.

Provan, Iain. *Ecclesiastes/Song of Songs.* NIV Application Commentary. Grand Rapids: Zondervan, 2001.

Rad, Gerhard von. *Genesis.* Translated by John H. Marks. Old Testament Library. Philadelphia: Westminster, 1961.

———. *Old Testament Theology.* Translated by D. M. G. Stalker. 2 vols. Old Testament Library. Louisville: Westminster John Knox, 2001.

———. *Weisheit in Israel.* Neukirchen: Neukirchener, 1970.

———. *Wisdom in Israel.* Translated by James D. Martin. Nashville: Abingdon, 1972.

Robinson, H. Wheeler. *Inspiration and Revelation in the Old Testament.* Oxford: Clarendon, 1946.

Rowley, H. H, ed. *The Old Testament and Modern Study.* Oxford: Clarendon, 1951.

Seow, Choon-Leong. *Ecclesiastes.* Anchor Bible 18C. New York: Doubleday, 1997.

Tamez, Elsa. *When the Horizons Close: Rereading Ecclesiastes.* Translated by Margaret Wilde. Maryknoll: Orbis, 2000.

Westermann, Claus. *Elements of Old Testament Theology.* Translated by Douglas W. Stott. Atlanta: John Knox, 1982.

———. *Handbook to the Old Testament.* Translated and edited by Robert H. Boyd. Minneapolis: Augsburg, 1967.

Whybray, R. N. "Qoheleth, Preacher of Joy." *Journal for the Study of the Old Testament* 23 (1982): 87-98.

Wilder, Thornton. "Our Town." In *A Treasury of the Theatre,* edited by John Gassner. New York: Simon and Schuster, 1951.